# St. Michael's Parish

## Celebrating 150-years in Fernandina Beach, Florida

# St. Michael's Parish

## Celebrating 150-years in Fernandina Beach, Florida

*Captain John A. Pulsinelli, USN (ret)*

*St. Michael's Parish*

*Celebrating 150-years in Fernandina Beach, Florida*

Copyright © 2021 by John Pulsinelli - All rights reserved.

This is a work of non-fiction, based on extensive research by the author.

No part of this book or text may be used or reproduced in any manner whatsoever without the publisher or copyright owner's written permission, except in the case of brief quotations embodied in critical articles and reviews. No part of this text may be reproduced, transmitted, downloaded, decompiled, reverse-engineered, or stored in or introduced into any information storage and retrieval system, in any form or by any means, whether electronic or mechanical, now known or invented in the future, without the express written permission of Giro di Mondo publishing services or the copyright holder.

Published by Giro di Mondo Publishing,
A subsidiary of The Ottima Group, LLC, of Fernandina Beach, Florida

www.girodimondo.com

Printed in the United States of America.

Cover by Roseanna White
Interior Design by Mark Fenn
Historical Photos and Images with permission of
Amelia Island Museum of History (AIMH)

FIRST EDITION (Hardcover print)
ISBNs: 978-1-7371388-4-6 (Hardcover)
978-1-7371388-5-3 (Paperback)
978-1-7371388-6-0 (Digital)
Library of Congress Control Number (LCCN): 2022930328

***St. Michael's Mission Statement***

*We are the body of Christ at St. Michael's Parish,*
*called to,*
*gather for worship; celebrate the Paschal Mysteries,*
*preach the Gospel,*
*minister to others and be witnesses to the world.*

*Illustration of the new church done by Heather Young*

# Table of Contents

<u>Chapter–</u> <u>Page</u>

Parish Mission Statement — v
1. A Rich History Surrounds Us. — 1
2. The birth of Catholicism in the New World — 6
3. A Spanish King's and French Queen's Missions Collide in La Florida — 12
4. A Nascent Catholic Community on Amelia Island — 18
5. The New Diocese and St. Michael's Parish Face Numerous challenges — 30
6. St. Michael's and the Catholic Church enter the Twentieth Century — 51
7. A New Millennium — 76
8. A Decade of Change, Challenges, and Opportunities — 89
9. Celebrating a Proud and Blessed Heritage, and laying a Solid Foundation for the Future — 112

St. Michael's Catholic Church Recorded Data — 115
Acknowledgments — 116
Bibliography of Material Reviewed — 118
Photo Credits — 123
Footnotes — 124

*Chapter One*

## A Rich History Surrounds Us

The Fernandina Beach community is surrounded by living history. Much of it lies within walking distance of the beautifully renovated and expanded St. Michael's Roman Catholic Church. Located within the Fernandez Reserve and in Villalonga Park, are the historic landmarks-- St. Michael's Academy (formerly St. Joseph's Academy and Convent), the old St. Peter Claver Church on the corner of Third and Calhoun Streets (now a private residence), former St. Peter Claver School on Calhoun between Fifth and Sixth Streets (currently home to St. Michael's Academy Kindergarten), the Phelan-Verot House on Fourth a half-block from the Church purchased by the first Bishop of the Diocese of St. Augustine Jean-Pierre Augustin Verot for the Sisters of Saint Joseph in February 1875.

From the Church, it is a short drive to San Carlos Plaza in Old Town Fernandina to find the first Spanish Missions, Santa Maria, established in 1566-1569. and the Spanish military garrison of Fort San Carlos built in 1816. Also nearby is the Bosque Bello Cemetery. In Bosque Bello lie the simply marked graves of the nineteen Sisters of St. Joseph and Father P.J. Halligan, who remains the longest-tenured pastor of St. Michael's church and parish, who served for seventeen years (1935-52).

The current pastor, Reverend Jose Kallukalam, ordained in Kerala, India, is the second longest-tenured pastor at nearly eleven years of service at St. Michael's (January 2011-Present). Father Jose who just celebrated his Jubilee Anniversary, has overseen the most dramatic expansion, renovations, and renewal of the church and parish in spiritual and temporal terms since the laying of its cornerstone on September 29, 1872. Father Jose insists that none of this would have been possible without the generous support of his parishioners, who gave freely of their time, talent, and treasure.

During his tenure, St. Michael's Catholic Church was expanded and underwent what has been described as a "magnificent, blended transformation" of old and new, maintaining the historical integrity of the Church while expanding it to accommodate the current seventeen hundred plus parish families. Accompanying the Church expansion was a much-needed enlarged parking capability. Also, during this time, a new Parish Hall was built in 2013. The historic Liberty Billings House (Green House) was relocated to Fifth and Broome Streets and completely restored. Church officials oversaw the construction and dedication of the Mission church and parish of St. Francis of Assisi in Yulee. If that were not enough, the parish purchased and executed a historic renovation of a new Parish Office and Administration facility directly across from the Church on the corner of Fourth and Broome streets. All this activity coincided with ongoing renovations at St. Michael's Academy.

During this unprecedented period, St. Michael's active parish membership experienced a major pastoral renewal with increasing outreach and participation in all family, service, and outreach ministries. Every aspect of parish involvement benefited from a commitment to take them from "good" to "great."

The parish was incredibly blessed to have the pastoral careers of Father Jose Kallukalam and Bishop Felipe J. Estevez overlap.

Bishop Estevez was named Bishop in June 2011 to oversee a flock of more than 160,000 Catholics in sixty-seven parishes, missions, and chapels across seventeen counties in the Diocese of St. Augustine. The diocese also boasts five high schools, thirty-three elementary schools, and early learning centers, including St. Michael's parish.

Bishop Estevez is the tenth Bishop of St. Augustine. He has been supporting, encouraging, and guiding St. Michael's Pastor, parish council, and parishioners through what has been an exciting and inspirational decade of growth and renewal. He also led the parish through some significant challenges, including leading the diocese through the COVID-19 pandemic—that still lingers at this writing.

It is also noteworthy that Bishop Estevez was born in Havana, Cuba, and ordained in the United States in May 1970. Bishop Estevez is the first Bishop of the Diocese of St. Augustine of Spanish/Cuban ancestry since the Parish of St. Augustine was first established more than 450 years ago. This parish was part of the Diocese of Santiago de Cuba led by Bishop Juan del Castillo (1564-1578). He has a doctorate from the Gregorian University in Rome and is fluent in English, Spanish, French, and Italian.

Bishop Estevez came to the United States on an Operation Pedro (Peter) Pan flight as a teenager. Parents fearing for their children's futures in Castro's communist Cuba participated with the Catholic Welfare Bureau to help execute a clandestine mass exodus of some 14,000 unaccompanied Cuban minors ages six to eighteen to the US over two years (1960-62). Many say that Bishop Estevez was sent to St. Augustine on a "wing and a prayer" by his caring parents and with the intervention of the Holy Spirit.

With all this in mind, today's parishioners are proud of their St. Michael's Catholic Church and its heritage that is traced to the founding and early settlement of St. Augustine on September 8, 1565, by General Pedro Menendez de Aviles for King Philip II of Spain. As most are aware, St. Augustine is the first permanent Catholic parish and settlement in the United States. St. Michael's parish can legitimately trace its beginnings to the Spanish Mission of Santa Maria on the Isle de Santa Maria (Amelia Island) some 450 years ago.

A portrait of Don Pedro Menéndez de Avíles, founder of St. Augustine in 1565, hangs in the Mission Nombre de Dios Museum.

*General Pedro Menéndez*

Captain John A. Pulsinelli, USN (ret)

## Chapter Two

## The birth of Catholicism in the New World

*In the Name of God*

The birth of Catholicism in the New World began with the planting of a Cross and the words "Nombre de Dios" [in the] "name of God,"

*Illustration of Nombre de Dios and first Mass*

marking the establishment of the first mission at the site of the first Catholic Parish Mass, in St. Augustine, Fl. The Mass was celebrated on the grounds by Father Francisco Lopez de Mendoza Grajales, Chaplain of the Menendez expedition, and four other priests. While it was the first established mission, others insist it was, by its very nature and purpose, the first parish and Father Francisco Lopez the "first pastor" in the continental United States. In his own written words, the priest stated that "As I had gone ashore the evening before, I took the Cross and went to meet him [the General] singing the hymn, Te Deum Laudamus [Latin: God, We Praise You]. The General, followed by all who accompanied him, marched up to the Cross, knelt, and kissed it. A large number of Indians watched these proceedings and imitated all they saw done."

*Father Lopez statue and Cross*

Today, the *Nombre de Dios* site is called the "Sacred Acre," a name given to the site reportedly by the late President John Fitzgerald Kennedy during one of his visits. It is home to the first Mass and the Chapel and Shrine of Our Lady of La Leche, the oldest Marian devotion in the United States. The Mission *Nombre de Dios* Museum and Prince of Peace Votive Church are also located there and are a must for a visit or pilgrimage.

Church records dating back to 1594 preserved in the Cathedral Basilica of St. Augustine's archives indicate St. Augustine's parish began its existence as a parish of the Diocese of Santiago de Cuba. The first permanent parish church in St. Augustine, Nuestra Senora de Los Remedios (Our Lady of Remedies) was built south of the Mission of Nombre de Dios in 1572. To offer some historical perspective, the permanent settlement and parish of St. Augustine predate the Plymouth colony by fifty years and the Jamestown settlement by thirty-five years.

While it is difficult to put an exact date on establishing the first mission on Amelia Island, Santa Maria, some historical documents indicate that General Pedro Menendez built a garrison on the Island as early as 1566-1569 to protect the Catholic missionaries and their native converts. Others suggest that the Mission of Santa Maria was in the area of Plaza San Carlos in "Old

Town" between 1597-1602. Regardless of which dates are most historically accurate, we can confidently state that the Mission of Santa Maria predates the Plymouth colony (1620) and the Jamestown settlement (1607).

We know that the Jesuit and Franciscan missionaries who followed the establishment of the parish mission were ministering

*Illustration of Mission Santa Maria*

to the needs of the Spanish colonists and engaged in the difficult task of evangelizing indigenous Mocama, Guale, and Timucuan natives. The Jesuit Priests arriving between 1566-1568 suffered martyrdom, and those who survived returned home in 1572. Many more Franciscan missionaries arrived in 1577 as part of a significant effort to convert the indigenous people to Christianity. Many of those suffered the same fate shortly after they arrived.

Of significance to St. Michael's history is that during the early Spanish colonial period, five Franciscan missionaries perished for their faith. They were converting and tending to the needs of the indigenous Guale Indians at their Santa Catalina mission located on St. Catherine's Island (Georgia) and later moved to the Isle de Santa Maria (Amelia Island). They were bludgeoned to death with war axes during a native people's uprising known as the "Juanilla revolt" in September 1597. It was prompted by a young chieftain, Juanilla, smarting from being reprimanded for adhering to his native practice of polygamy.

> Among those martyred in September 1597 was a Franciscan missionary, Father Miguel de Aunon, for whom St. Michael's Catholic Church was dedicated under the patronage of St. Michael the Archangel on September 29, 1872, St. Michael the Archangel's feast day.

Father Miguel and his lay assistant, Brother Antonio de Badajoz, were martyred on September 19, 1597, at Mission Santa Catalina, the northernmost and newest established Spanish Mission on the barrier islands. As the story goes, local Christian Guale natives warned Brother Antonio. They offered safe passage for the two missionaries to Cumberland Island, but he refused to believe the threat was real.

*Fray Miguel and Brother Antonio*

St. Michael's Church was built and dedicated by Father Joannes Bertazzi, the second permanent Pastor who served from 1870-1879. Father Bertazzi's remains are buried in front of St. Michael's church beside the grave of Father Carolus Sartorio. Father Sartorio was the first permanent Pastor of St. Michael's parish 1869-1870, and died at age twenty-seven, a year after arriving. Father Sartorio's pastorate began in February 1869 and ended in July 1870 with his untimely death. However, he added eighty-six new parishioners during that time, most of them through baptisms as documented in St. Michael's Baptism Register.

> *"And when the Lamb opened the fifth seal, I saw under the altar the souls of those who had been slain for the word of God and for the testimony they had upheld."* Revelation 6:9

## Chapter 3

## A Spanish King's and French Queen's Missions Collide in La Florida

Another well-known piece of history is that of other Christian neighbors. Under Jean Ribault's leadership, the French Huguenots were the first to establish a permanent settlement at Fort Caroline in May 1562. This is some twenty-five miles north of St. Augustine on the St. John's River, and named the Island the Isle de Mai (after the month they landed). However, their presence was short-lived, resulting in the first conflict between European powers in La Florida and the New World. Spain's King Philip II was not happy with what he considered the encroachment on territory that Spain felt was its own. He reasoned that after all, Juan Ponce de Leon arrived in 1513 and mapped the entire coast of La Florida, from the St. John's River to Mobile Bay. Shortly after returning to Florida in 1521 with diocesan priests and missionaries, he was mortally wounded with an arrow owned by local natives.

Hernando de Soto landed near Tampa in 1539 with secular priests and Dominican Friars. Dominican Father Louis Cancer de Barbastro joined them in Tampa in 1549 only to be beaten to death by local natives.

In 1559, Don Tristan de Luna arrived in Pensacola Bay with an expedition of five hundred soldiers, one thousand colonists, and six Dominican priests, but that settlement was short-lived. While none of these attempts at colonization were successful, King Philip was not amused by what he considered the French intrusion.

The rest of this period's story is among the greatest ironies in the history of Catholicism in the New World and the Diocese of St. Augustine. The entrenched Huguenots were sent to La Florida by the Catholic Queen and Regent of France, Catherine de Medici, because she felt the Huguenots were threatening her control of her predominantly Catholic country. Catherine believed that she could rid herself of the problem by sending the Huguenots to explore, claim, and colonize the vast territory of La Florida.

The Huguenots' challenge to Catherine in France ultimately led to the French wars of religion (1562-1598) between Catholics and Calvinist Huguenots. It also found its way to the New World and the newly established Catholic Settlement of St. Augustine.

The presence of the French Huguenots greatly troubled the King of Spain. He sent one of his most experienced and loyal Generals [also described as one of the most 'ruthless'] Pedro Menendez de Aviles to 'reclaim' La Florida for the Spanish crown.

The battle that ensued resulted in the French losing Fort Caroline and Ribault and most of their fleet in a storm. Less than a dozen Catholic sailors survived. Other survivors were massacred on September 19, 1565, in Matanzas Bay. The Spanish word *matanzas* means "slaughters" and therefore it was the name given to the bay. Some local historians believe that the first encounter between the Spanish and French Fleets occurred in Cumberland Sound. Others speculate that Fort Caroline was located at Roses Bluff overlooking Cumberland Sound and the St. Mary and Amelia Rivers. Regardless, this battle helped secure Spanish control of Florida for the next two hundred thirty-five years, with several interruptions mainly by the British and some pirates along the way.

In the 1600s, there were at least three Spanish Missions and possibly four on Amelia Island. In addition to the Mission of Santa Maria already located on Amelia Island, the northernmost missions of Santa Maria de Yamasee and Santa Catalina de Guale were relocated to Amelia Island by the Spanish from the coast of Georgia. This consolidation and general retreat of the missions in 1680 was due to increasingly aggressive attacks by the British and their Indian allies. According to archaeologist Ripley Bullen, this occurred somewhere between 1675-1696, when the missions were moved to the South end of the Island in what would become the Harrison Plantation and the resort community of Amelia Island Plantation. When Samuel Harrison built his homestead in 1790, his main house was erected on one of the missions' cemeteries. Almost two hundred years later, during the construction of Dr. and Mrs. Dorian's house on Amelia Island Plantation in the 1980s, the remains of a mission were unearthed. Archaeologists describe the Harrison homestead associated with the Santa Maria and Santa Catalina missions on the leeward side of Amelia Island as ideal environmental sites---centrally located on a barrier island with access to the Amelia River and fresh spring water---with obvious advantages for both supply and defense.

According to the John B. Stetson Collection--an extensive collection of documents that cover Florida's Spanish colonial history with an emphasis on the rise and fall of the mission system-there was also a San Pedro de Tropique mission on the Island.

A photographic reproduction of a mission and fort that existed in 1690 with four bastions and a Church was included in Governor Zuniga's letter to the Spanish Crown on November 5, 1702. While its exact location has still not been determined, it may also have been associated with the Spanish watch house built on the site of the Plaza San Carlos in 1696 in Old Town. The general time frame for these events seems reasonable since it has been determined that the first commercial or military settlement of Fernandina was in 1680 when the Spaniards established a secondary base here for military and naval operations. Because of its military importance overlooking the inlet to the natural deep-water harbor and future port of Fernandina, the Spanish returned and built Fort San Carlos in 1816.

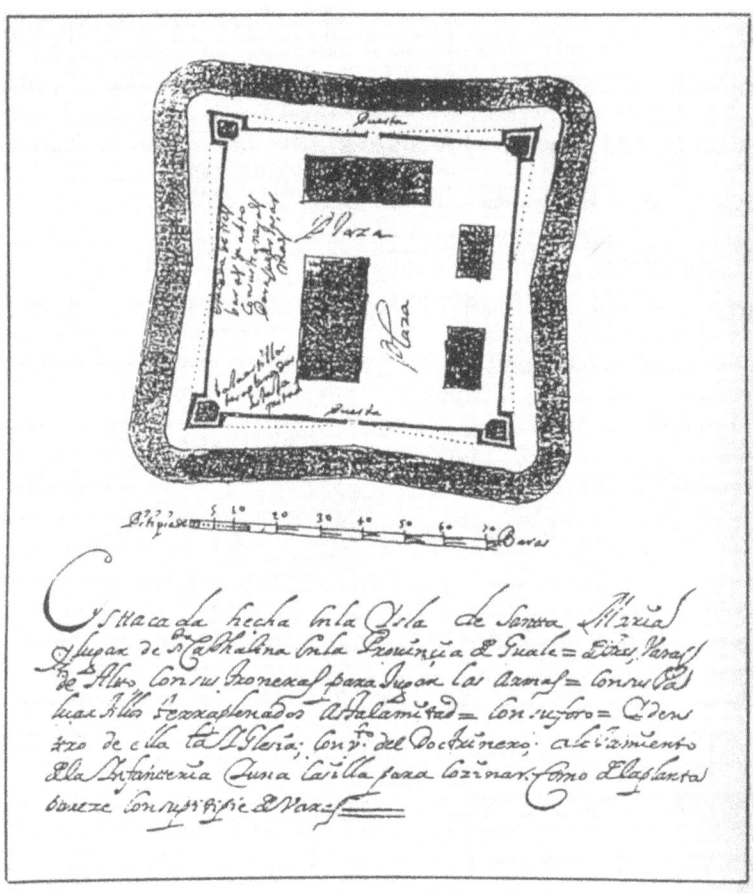

*Mission Santa Maria with 4 bastions and the church in the middle of the mission.*

In 1634, the Franciscan province of St. Helena, with a motherhouse in St. Augustine, contained forty-four missions, thirty-five missionaries, and thirty thousand Roman Catholic Native Americans. By 1702, the British had destroyed all Spanish Missions from the Carolinas to St. Augustine, with only the Mission *Nombre de Dios* surviving. During the periods of British occupation, the church suffered severe setbacks, and almost all vestiges of the Catholic faith disappeared.

*Chapter Four*

## A Nascent Catholic Community on Amelia Island

The British maintained a garrison from 1736 to 1742 on the island we know as Amelia. The island was named by Georgia's founder and British colonial Governor James Oglethorpe in honor of the daughter of Great Britain's King George II in 1742. When the British returned in 1763 (following the Treaty of Paris that ended the seven Year's War between Britain and France) Spain traded Florida to regain control of Cuba. The Earl of Egmont's Indigo Plantation encompassed most of the Island. For some twenty years, Amelia was also known as "Egmont Island" as referenced on the historic marker in front of Villalonga Park. However, despite his large land holdings, the second Earl of Egmont (John Parseval) never set foot on Amelia. He had only recently begun his plan for the development of the Island that he would call Amelia Egmont Island, and Old Town Fernandina was to be called Egmont town. At the time of his death in 1770, his wife the countess, hired Stephen Egan to manage the estate's affairs and follow through with

Egmont's plans, but the plantation was later raided and destroyed by American troops from Georgia during the Revolution (1775-1783).

> **FERNANDEZ GRANT**
>
> During the Spanish and English periods of Florida history, many large tracts of land were granted primarily to induce settlement. All that remains of the Don Domingo Fernandez Spanish Grant is the family cemetery and this park. Royal title to this property was granted August 9, 1807. This land was once a part of the Earl of Egmont property on Amelia Island, which included the present site of the City of Fernandina Beach.

*Historic Marker in Villalonga Park*

Although the British Crown guaranteed freedom of religion, there was a general exodus of Roman Catholic settlers during this period. This included about five hundred survivors out of about fourteen hundred Catholics "recruited" from Mediterranean lands in 1768. They came as indentured slaves brought to Florida to support what was called the British Turnbull colony in New Smyrna. When their indentured status was over in 1777, the few remaining Roman Catholics settled in St. Augustine or moved to towns like Jacksonville, Fernandina, Tampa, and Key West, forming part of the nucleus of Catholic congregations there.

In 1783, the Second Treaty of Paris, both ended the Revolutionary War and returned Florida to Spain. There is no question Amelia Island was discovered and settled early in America's history. Successive waves of French, Spanish and English nationals explored its surrounding waters and colonized its strategic harbor and fertile land in the sixteenth, seventeenth, eighteenth, and nineteenth centuries. The history of Amelia Island and what later became the town of Fernandina can historically be described as a crucible where world events converged, and European/world powers of the day competed and fought over the ownership rights of this barrier island and its surroundings.

*Canon on Plaza San Carlos site of former Fort*

For a short time, Loyalists who had escaped Charleston and Savannah during the close of the American Revolution came to the Island and named what would become Old Town Fernandina, Hillsborough. It and the Amelia harbor became an embarkation point for Loyalists to leave the colonies; they tore down buildings and took the lumber to Britain. In June 1785, former British governor Patrick Toyn moved his command to Hillsborough town, from where he sailed to England and evacuated troops and Loyalists later that year.

Fernandina initially grew slowly into a disorderly "wild west" town during the latter years of the American Revolution. She was renamed Fernandina by the Spanish in 1785 in honor of Spanish King Ferdinand VII. It became the focal settlement of a growing population with its history inextricably tied to the growth of the Catholic Church in the New World. Fernandina can lay claim to being one of the oldest settlements in the continental United States, and St. Michaels one of the first Catholic parishes established in the 'diocese' of St. Augustine with the parish of St. Augustine having rightful claim as the first.

While the actual building of St. Michaels church was still a long way off, Church records and census indicate that by 1783 there were one hundred and three Catholic families on Amelia Island, most of them baptized in the Amelia River.

According to a historical sketch written by Father Edward Booth, who served as St. Michael's pastor from 1983 to 1988, King Charles III sent Father Hassett and Father O'Reilly to Florida as early as 1778. Charles paid the two priests' expenses and provided them with a yearly salary to rekindle the Catholic faith. He commanded them to obtain support from the Bishop of Santiago de Cuba, whose jurisdiction comprised Florida. When the priests arrived in St. Augustine in 1784, most signs of Catholicism had disappeared---the convent turned into a barracks, the Church swept away in a storm. No trace of the once flourishing missions existed.

However, two parishes were established along the St. John's and St. Mary's River, with clergy assigned to each. These may have been the early vestiges of the Immaculate Conception Parish in Jacksonville and St. Michaels/St. Peter Claver's parish in Fernandina.

At St. Augustine, there is a record of the baptisms performed by Father Hassett on his trip through the northern part of the 'diocese' on the St. John's and St. Mary's Rivers and Talbot Isle during the years 1784-1792. Father Hassett performed about twenty Baptisms along the Amelia River area in 1790. In 1791, the Franciscans who had served the parishes on the St. John's and St. Mary's Rivers were recalled. In the absence of Franciscan missionaries, three Irish priests, Father Barry, Father Cosby, and Father Wallis, following their instruction, proceeded to St. Augustine to serve the needs of those two and other outlying parishes

Pope Pius VI established the Diocese of Louisiana and the Floridas in 1793. The Right Reverend Luis Penalver served as its first Bishop with residence in New Orleans. Following Bishop Penalver's promotion and departure in 1801, Reverend Thomas Hassett was made Administrator of the Vicariate for a short time. (A vicariate is territorial jurisdiction of the Catholic Church under a titular bishop centered in missionary regions and countries where dioceses or parishes have not yet been established.)

In 1806, the Vicariate and parishes of Florida came under the first Bishop of Baltimore, the renowned Bishop Carroll. Then, the Bishops of Havana reassumed authority over Florida until the appointment of Reverend Michael Portier in 1825 as the first and only Bishop of the new Vicariate of Alabama and Florida.

In 1811, Catholics on Amelia Island were visited and ministered to by priests from St. Augustine who traveled by horse or mule to their parishioners. In 1814, the people requested a chapel and a resident priest, but the authorities provided neither. A publication by the Reverend Michael J. Curley, CSSR, *Church, and State in the Spanish Floridas (1783-1822),* indicates that the Bishop of Havana, Bishop Espada, appealed to the Captain-General of Cuba for funds to erect a chapel at Fernandina, but the Captain-General denied the request.

In 1827, as the 'diocese' grew, the need for priests became critical, and Bishop Portier made an earnest appeal for assistance. The Reverend Edward D. Mayne, Vicar General from Mount St. Mary Seminary in Emmitsburg, Maryland, was sent to St. Augustine. The able-bodied priest labored zealously in the city and across the scattered stations on the coast as far north as Amelia Island and Fernandina. In 1839, the mission in Fernandina, apparently still without a church, was attended by Father Patrick Hackett from Mobile and Father Claude Rampon from St.

Augustine. According to Michael V. Gannon's book, *The Cross in the Sand*, a small mission church was built in Fernandina around the year 1844 in what is now Old Town Fernandina with Father Edmund Aubril in "residence." The term residence here probably does not mean permanent, but rather the priest assigned from St. Augustine ministered to the parish's needs regularly.

During the early-mid-nineteenth century, the trade of Fernandina developed so rapidly that in 1811 the Governor of the Spanish province of East Florida, Enrique White, ordered surveyor General George Clarke to replot the town. It is worth noting that in 2011 the city of Fernandina celebrated its Bicentennial Anniversary 1811-2011. A bench on the Plaza San Carlos in Old town Fernandina commemorates this historic event, with Fernandina becoming the last Spanish city plotted in the Western Hemisphere. On January 1, 1825, Fernandina became incorporated. Little development ensued in the town until 1853 when the Florida Railroad Company and its President and first Florida Senator David Yulee announced Fernandina would form the eastern terminus for the first Cross-state railroad in Florida.

It was in the replotting of Fernandina that we find the Church lots five and seven of block two referred to in Reverend Ed Booth's historical sketch as "Church lots one and two directly across the street from Fort San Carlos." In the transfer of governments from Spain to Britain in 1763, the Church lost ownership of the property. However, in 1867. Bishop Verot, then Vicar Apostolic of the Florida

## St. Michael's Parish

Vicariate, repurchased the church lots in Old Town and built a chapel for Catholic families living there.

The green historical marker between the St. Michael's Church and St. Michael's Academy describes the Spanish Land Grant to Don Domingo Fernandez in 1807 and the former Egmont estate. The other side tells the story about the Florida Railroad Company and the growth of Fernandina in the mid-nineteenth century. The heirs of Don Domingo Fernandez sold David Yulee all the land where the current city of Fernandina now stands for $10 an acre. All that remains of the Spanish Land Grant awarded to Don

*St Michael's children reenacting colonial MAYPOLE dance during Mayday celebrations in Villalonga Park*

Domingo Fernandez is the Fernandez Reserve where St. Michael's Church and St. Michael's Academy stand, and the Fernandez cemetery site within Villalonga Park. The Park is all that remains of what was then called Yellow Bluff and Eliza (or Louisa) Plantations.

The home of Don Domingo and his wife Maria (Mattair), who were married there in Dec 1793, is across the street. Maria had inherited considerable land holdings from her mother [Mary Mattair] that included one-hundred-fifty acres in what is now 'Old Town.' Don Domingo Fernandez, who worked as a harbor pilot on the Amelia River and gunboat captain for the Spanish government until 1800, was probably awarded the grants in 1807 for his service and loyalty to the Spanish Crown. Following retirement in 1800, he became a prominent planter. The Fernandez grant extended West as far as the Amelia River. Jane, their youngest daughter, married John Villalonga against her parents' wishes. John was a poor Spanish immigrant who worked on her father's plantation. However, John would eventually make his own fortunes in cotton before and after the Civil War. The Villalonga family's youngest daughter, Leonilla, or Ms. "Nilla," as she was affectionately called by those who knew her, contributed heavily to the construction of St. Michael's Church and St. Joseph's Academy and Convent. Nilla donated the Italian marble altars in both the convent chapel and St. Michael's church with marble taken from the same quarry in northern Italy that

*Leonilla in Villalonga Park*

Michelangelo used to create his masterpiece, The Pietà. There was also an unconfirmed report claiming that embedded in the Church altar is a piece of wood believed by the Catholic Church to be a class one relic of the True Cross.

*The current altar decorated for Christmas*

*Oldest photo of interior of church with altar decorated for Palm Sunday.*

Ms. Villalonga also built the house across the street from the Church on the corner of Fourth and Broome Streets, for her musical protégé and adopted niece Miss Edith Gordon, married Hood, which now serves as the renovated parish office. Edith previously lived with and was raised by her aunt Ms. Leonilla Villalonga in an apartment for Ms. Nilla above the Sisters of St. Joseph Convent kitchen. When Ms. Edith reached her teens, the apartment became too confining for her teenage activities, and Ms. Villalonga built a house for her to freely practice her music and entertain.

*Mrs. Edith Gordon Hood in Villalonga Park*

Ms. Nilla never married, lived to be 72, and was the last member of the family to be buried in the Fernandez family cemetery on August 15, 1915. She and her family were without question the most prominent benefactors of their day at St. Michael's church and parish.

*Chapter Five*

## The New Diocese and St. Michael's Parish Face Numerous challenges

It was not until 1850 that the See of Savannah was erected into a diocese by Pope Pius IX. This included part of Florida east of the Apalachicola River and constituted as a separate Vicariate in 1857 under the Right Reverend Augustin Verot as Vicar Apostolic.

*Bishop Verot*

## St. Michael's Parish

In 1870, Bishop Verot became the first Bishop of the Diocese of St. Augustine, when the Vicariate was elevated to the Diocese of St. Augustine.

When the vicariate was established in 1857, Reverend E. Aubril and Reverend S. Sheridan were at St. Augustine, and there were chapels at the stations at Black Creek, Fernandina (the Church/chapel built in Old Town in 1844) and St. John's Beach, and one being constructed at Palatka (St. Monica). The Catholics at these locations were ministered to by Father Aubril and Father Madeore.

Bishop Verot entered his difficult pastorate with extraordinary zeal and activity. He visited Europe in May 1859 in need of more priests and **religious** and returned with six priests, four Brothers of the Christian Schools, and Religious Sisters of Mercy. During that period, he helped build a Church in Mandarin; rebuild a Church destroyed in a hurricane in Mayport; restore the ancient shrine of Our Lady de la Leche at *Nombre de Dios* and established missions at various points throughout the state.

After centuries of Spanish rule, more than twenty years of British occupation, and twenty-five years as a US Territory, Florida became the twenty-seventh state of the United States on March 3, 1845.

*The Metropolitan Catholic Almanac* for 1859 states, "Fernandina is a rapidly growing town where there is a Church in the progress of erection; it is attended once a month from

Jacksonville and St. Augustine." It also references parish baptismal records beginning February 29, 1860, reflecting Baptisms by two of Bishop Verot's priests Reverend E. Hillaire and Father John Bernard Aulance.

The early Church faced many challenges, not the least of which was the ravages of war---the Civil War [1861-1865]. From October 1861-February 1862, the Reverend Henry P. Clavreul, a native of Le Puy, France, was stationed at Fernandina assisting as Chaplain to a garrison of two thousand confederate recruits.

*Reverend Henry P. Clavreul*

He was also the priest in charge of the Catholic Church on March 2, 1862, when Union troops took military possession of the island. He had been recruited by Bishop Verot during Bishop Verot's trip home to Le Puy in May 1859. For several years, Reverend Clavreul was the visitant priest to Fernandina, traveling there by mule until 1877. Reverend Clavreul records in his Diary, "From 1867 to 1877, residing in St. Augustine a great part of the time, I had also now and again temporary charge of Fernandina." Additional visiting priests during this period---Fathers Mailley, Delafosse, and Landry--- recorded Baptisms, marriages, first communions, and deaths in parish records. A. M. Delafosse administered a Baptism on May 5, 1866, in "new" Fernandina.

Union troops broke into the Catholic Church shortly after their occupation in 1862 and stole "vestments and a sacred vessel."

*Union Troops Occupying Fernandina March 3, 1862*

This act so infuriated Reverend Clavreul that he slipped through Union lines to report the incident to Bishop Verot in Savannah, who issued a strong letter protesting the vandalism and theft to the first Union officers he could collar. While he got the attention of local senior Union officers, it is unknown if they caught or punished the culprits or if the stolen items were returned.

Author Michael Gannon, a former priest who served briefly at St. Michael's Church in the summer of 1961, provides a vivid biographical portrait of Bishop Verot in his book *"Rebel Bishop."* The title was given to him by his northern counterparts. Notwithstanding Verot's enthusiastic support of southern principles, he had vast sympathy for Union prisoners at the notorious Andersonville prison in Georgia. Reverend Clavreul was one of his priests who he sent to minister to the needs and alleviate some of the unspeakable suffering of the prisoners during the war. In his book, *The Cross in the Sand,* Gannon states that he sent five priests to enter the compound and minister among its horrors." Verot himself visited the prison twice. Throughout the war, Bishop Verot bore enormous responsibility for both his Georgia and Florida vicariates, crossing Union lines on countless occasions to care for the safety and well-being of his priests, nuns, and parishioners.

Thus, in 1859, a long association began between the early St. Michael's Church and the first Bishop of Florida-- Jeanne-Pierre Augustin Verot. He visited all the chapels and churches in his widespread vicariate and was sensitive to their needs. Through his efforts and the recruiting of his French priests, missionaries, and the Sisters of Saint Joseph, who came to America in 1866 and began their local service in 1871, a close bond developed between the Catholic community of Fernandina, Florida, and Le Puy, France.

The bishop appears to have been a man preordained to take hold of the leadership of the Catholic Church in Florida at a time of early rapid development, periods of great social unrest and turmoil, and the Civil War. Bishop Verot also began his apostolic work among the freed slaves in Fernandina purchasing lots and ordering the building of a Catholic Church in Old Town in 1867 for the thirty or so African American Catholic families living there. In Bishop Verot's "Record," beginning September 1867, he wrote, "I went to Fernandina where I spent a few days and bought back the Church lot of Old Fernandina, which had been lost during the war, and gave orders for a little chapel for the [African American Catholics] in the Old Town." This was later rebuilt in 1895 during Father Anthony Kilcoyne's pastorate and became St. Peter Claver Catholic Church for the black parishioners. It was named after Saint Peter Claver, canonized in 1888 for his missionary work among slaves. Bishop Verot's devoted attention to the Roman Catholic congregations on Amelia Island and throughout the diocese ended only with his death on June 10, 1876.

St. Michael's church Centennial history documents that the present sanctuary built in 1872 replaced a wooden-structured church erected in 1859 which was located on the site of the current church until sometime in 1871. That history also credits Irish laborers engaged in constructing Yulee's Florida Coastal Railroad for their substantial contributions to the building of the earlier church. The Catholic Church may also be mentioned in a Letter from Fernandina, Florida published on 1 March 1865, in the Boston Semi-Weekly Advertiser as "an unpretending building standing near the Domingo Fernandez grave monument."

According to *The Florida Catholic*, the first two permanent Pastors of St. Michael's Roman Catholic Church were Italian priests. Father Carolus Sartorio arrived in February 1869 at the age of twenty-six. Father Sartorio served only one year due to his premature death in July 1870. Succeeding Father Sartorio in 1870 was Father Johannes Bertazzi, who arrived in Savannah from Genoa, Italy, in 1868, came to St. Michael's and served until he died

*The gravestones in front of the Church*

in 1879. Similar gravestones mark the final resting place of both pioneer priests in front of the Church at the Northeast corner behind a small brick wall.

During Father Bertazzi's Ministry, St. Michael's church and sanctuary were built and dedicated, with a cornerstone laid on September 29, 1872. During Father Bertazzi's pastorate, the first Sisters of Saint Joseph---Sister Marie Celenie Joubert and novice Sister Helen--- came to Fernandina to prepare the congregation's children for their First Holy Communion. They earned such great

*The One Room Schoolhouse behind the Church*

admiration from the Catholic community that they were asked and allowed to stay and continue their teaching. Initially, the Sisters lived and taught in two small rooms at the rear of the Church, which was still a wooden structure. They ate, slept, and taught there. Lacking cooking facilities, the parents and families of their students provided their meals.

A small cottage nearby was eventually rented for them on the Wilson estate on the corner of Eighth and Broome in 1871. Four more Sisters from the Jacksonville convent joined to help them with classes in 1874. According to a presentation by George T. Davis in October 1992 to the Amelia Island Museum of History, they may have also lived and taught in a cottage at 210 North Third St. between Broome and Calhoun. His was the only reference associating the Sisters with this cottage which still stands there. During one of his visits in 1875, according to his "*Record,*" Bishop Verot, upon seeing the inadequate lodging of the nuns, bought them a house at 116 North Fourth Street about half a block south of St. Michael's church, the Phelan-Verot House. There is a historical marker in front of that residence. The Sisters of St. Joseph lived there during the Yellow Fever Epidemic of 1877 and the construction of St. Joseph's Academy and Convent. The Phelan-Verot House was nicknamed the "Needle House" because, during the epidemic, local women would throw their balls of thread with needles on the front porch for the Sisters to use to sew together the numerous burlap and canvas bags to bury the dead.

*Phelan-Verot House*

Bishop Verot contributed substantially "financially and spiritually" to building St. Michael's. In his "Record," he also writes, "In October 1872, I went from Tallahassee to Fernandina, where a new brick Church is being erected, and I gave direction for the continuing for the Church...in the Spring of 1873, I gave Confirmation at Fernandina where I saw the new Church that had been opened to divine worship on the eighth of February of the same year, is now completed."

According to *Sadler's Catholic Directory Almanac and Ordo* published in 1877, Reverend Augustine Spondonari was Administrator at St. Michael's. It recorded that, "the Catholics in Fernandina have succeeded in building a new and substantial brick

Church, which with its steeple and stained-glass windows does great honor to their taste and generosity. It has been dedicated to God, under the patronage of St. Michael, in remembrance of Father Michael de Aunon, who suffered martyrdom in this place at the time of the Indian rebellion against the Catholic clergy. On the Cornerstone of St. Michael's, it reads, September 29, 1872."

The church is described in a town survey much later as a "two-story masonry vernacular religious building, noteworthy for its gable roof with triangular parapets, rounded arch windows with a label with corbeled brick work and pilasters. It was the first building constructed of brick in the downtown area. It has been significantly altered by the replacement of original windows and porch and was remodeled in 1888--it was surfaced in stucco many

*Oldest photo of St. Michael's Church with a Picket fence and church steeple. This was before the rectory was built in 1879-1880*

years later when the bell tower was added to the northwest corner of the Church around 1924."

While much is written about the heroism and holy sacrifice of the Sisters of St. Joseph in caring for the victims of the Yellow Fever epidemic of 1877, little is written about Father Spondonari's indiscriminate care for the sick. Working side-by-side with the sisters of St. Joseph, he fell ill himself in September 1877, the month that the fever seized Fernandina. When Father J.L. Hugon of Tallahassee heard of the illness, he obtained permission from his bishop and proceeded to Fernandina to assist Father Spondonari. He found him still quite sick but out of danger, tending to the corporal and spiritual needs of the sick along with the Sisters and administering the sacraments to the dying with two of the five Sisters near death.

Sister Helen de Sales, at age twenty-six and Sister Celenie, at age thirty-three, became victims of the relentless disease and died within eight hours of each other; Sister de Sales, September twenty-first, and Sister Celenie, September twenty-second. The Sisters were granted permission from the mayor of Fernandina to bury them in the churchyard of St. Michael's in Villalonga Park as the two had requested. Some twenty years later, they were moved to Bosque Bello Cemetery. According to several historical accounts, Mr. Robert Henderson, county sexton, a respected member of St. Peter's Episcopal church, exhumed the bodies.

*Graves of Sisters Celenie and de Sales in Bosque Bello*

According to his personal report, when he opened the coffins for identification purposes, he stated that the Sisters' bodies were uncorrupted and that an aroma of roses came out from their coffins. The Catholic Church considers these signs of saintliness. All the other Sisters who contracted the disease recovered and lived.

According to George T. Davis, his grandfather, Dr. Theodore Starbach, a non-Catholic from Savannah, volunteered his services to assist the sick and dying. The Sisters of St. Joseph so inspired him that he felt compelled to say---"You have more valor and courage than the soldier on the battlefield…you go to meet death passing through the hardest trials, ….in order that you may relieve suffering humanity." The same doctor was so inspired by the faith and love of these "Angels of Mercy" that he converted to the Catholic faith. He died in the arms of Sister Marie Louise, whom he had labored with side-by-side for so many weeks nursing the sick, assisting the dying, and burying the dead. During the "Yellow Jack" epidemic in 1877, Fernandina was quarantined with approximately sixteen hundred permanent residents, including some three hundred Catholics. Over one thousand people contracted the disease. Though most recovered, there were ninety-four recorded deaths.

*Illustration of the Sisters nursing the sick*

It is a well-established fact that the Sisters of Saint Joseph hold a very endearing place in the history of the Church and the hearts and minds of the Fernandina community. These "Angels of Mercy" nursed the sick and dying during the Yellow Fever epidemic of 1877, as it is recorded beautifully in detail in Sister Catherine Byrne's handwritten notebook in their archives in St. Augustine and personal anecdotal stories shared by Captain George T. Davis. A one-room schoolhouse grew to become a highly respected Academy where boys and girls learned to prepare for the future. The Sisters of St. Joseph stayed and joined together with Amelia Island families to build a community treasure known as St. Joseph's Academy and Convent to teach Catholic and Protestant, black and white alike with a dedication and sweet discipline that all loved and cherished.

Sister Noelie was one of the first Sisters to establish the St. Joseph Convent in Fernandina with the cornerstone for the Motherhouse and St. Joseph's Academy laid on January 15, 1874.

*Aerial view of the Academy and Chapel and Villalonga Park*

St. Joseph's Academy held its first session in the fall of 1882 and throughout the years, religious and Catholic lay teachers have taught as much about moral and spiritual values as they did about language, math, and the arts.

> *"Let the little children come to me. Do not stop them, for it is to such as these that the Kingdom of God belongs"*
> **Mark 10:14**

As previously noted, in 1867, Bishop Verot wrote in his record that he went to Fernandina to buy back the Church lots in Old Fernandina lost during the war and ordered that a chapel be built for the African American Catholics in the parish. According to the archives, the inadequate original chapel was rebuilt in 1895 by St. Michael's pastor Father Anthony Kilcoyne and was described as "a handsome chapel" for Catholics living there. Many of the

*St. Peter Claver chapel is the building in the far right of the photo*

researched documents indicate that in Fernandina, the Catholic African American freed slaves had a flourishing congregation and the Sisters of St. Joseph opened schools not only in Fernandina, but also in St. Augustine and Jacksonville.

In 1879, the Right Reverend John Moore, second Bishop of St. Augustine, appointed Reverend John O'Boyle the successor to Father Bertazzi and Administrator Father Spondonari. Father O'Boyle erected a beautiful double galleried parochial residence, typical of the fine low country coastal dwellings of Amelia on the southeast corner of the Church block. This would have been directly behind the Church and can be clearly seen in one of the photos discovered in the archives.

*Double galleried parochial residence demolished in 1978.*

A new single-story ranch style home was purchased in 1976 on the opposite corner of Fifth and Broome as the new rectory and office. Anyone who became a parishioner here before 2019 would have met the legendary parish Secretary Jeanne Dean who would have greeted you and welcomed you with a big smile. The old double galleried parochial residence was in disrepair and was demolished in 1978.

Father O'Boyle, while not robust physically, was a beloved minister with missionary zeal who frequently visited the camps of Irish Catholics living in tents and shanties working on Yulee's Florida Atlantic Coast Line. He traveled by river ferry where Highway US 1 now crosses the St. Mary's River and from there walked a mile or more to the men's camps to tend to their spiritual needs. In Ms. Kate Tracy Dunbar's communications in Reverend Father Benedict Roth's history describing *"Boulogne of By-Gone Days,"* "Father O'Boyle heard confessions and said Mass by the side of stumps and logs." Father O'Boyle died at the age of ninety in Daytona Beach and is known as the "patriarch of diocesan clergy."

Father Anthony F.J. Kilcoyne, a mine boy from Scranton, Pennsylvania, graduated from St. Vincent Theological Seminary, Beatty [Latrobe], Pennsylvania and shepherded his flock at St. Michaels from 1884 until shortly before his death at age thirty-seven in June 1896.

Father Kilcoyne is best remembered for repairing and improving St. Michael's church in 1888 to virtually make it a

THE LATE REV. A. T. KILLCOYNE, OF SCRANTON.

"new Church" and in 1895 he built the handsome St. Peter Claver Chapel in Old Town for African American parishioners living there. His obituary read, "There is sorrow in every home today where the young priest was known…we have watched him rise from the humble position of mine boy to one of the most distinguished clergymen of the South." The ministers of the solemn high Mass of Requiem at St. Michael's were the Reverend William J. Kenny, vicar general of the diocese representing the Right Reverend Bishop

*Interior of Church 1884-1895*

Moore as the celebrant, the Reverend Father Maurice Foley, successor to the late Father Kilcoyne in charge of St. Michael's Church as Deacon, and Reverend John O'Brian as sub-deacon.

The close of the century brought us the Spanish-American War in 1898. As it was, Father Maurice Foley served his pastorate at St. Michaels From 1896 until 1903 when he was appointed Rector of the Cathedral of St. Augustine. Father Foley was Pastor at St. Michaels during the Spanish-American War when he and parishioners of St. Michael's cared for the spiritual and corporal needs of the Catholic soldiers of the sixty-ninth New York and eighth Michigan regiments camped at Fernandina. Father Foley was described in the 1900 New Year's edition of the *Florida Mirror* as a "most devout, pious, and learned divine pastor of the largest congregation in Fernandina." As a result of that conflict, the US acquired all of Spain's Pacific possessions, including the Philippines. Reverend Foley was later consecrated Bishop in 1910 at St. Augustine and became Bishop of Tuguegarao and Jaro, in the Philippines, where he died.

*Chapter Six*

## St. Michael's and the Catholic Church enter the Twentieth Century

An era of progress as it was referred to by Bishop Verot continued under the administration of Bishop John Moore (1877-1901) and his successor the Right Reverend William John Kenny, who Cardinal Gibbons consecrated in May 1902 in the Cathedral Basilica of St. Augustine. The Great Fire destroyed most of Jacksonville in 1901, including St. Mary's Home for Children established in 1886 and the Immaculate Conception Parish. In 1903, the pastoral charge of St. Michael's was assumed by Reverend John O'Brian. In 1911 he was also called to the rectorship of the Cathedral and simultaneously assumed the position of Vicar General of the Diocese of St. Augustine. He replaced the Very Reverend Henry P. Clavreul, one of the many French priests mentioned in this history that Bishop Verot brought to America during his tenure as Bishop of the Diocese of St. Augustine.

According to a census in 1907 and historical documents in 1924, the Catholic population on Amelia Island was over 400, with 125 African Americans. Like most of Florida's congregations, St. Michael's was principally composed of poor people, with *The Florida Catholic* publication reporting that the annual statements for the year 1906 amounted to $1,969. Nevertheless, St. Michael's church, St. Joseph's Academy and Convent, hosted many community events and galas in Villalonga Park including arts and craft fairs and concerts. These events featured Sister Noelie's accomplished student musicians and the famous lace, jams, and jellies made by the Sisters of St. Joseph.

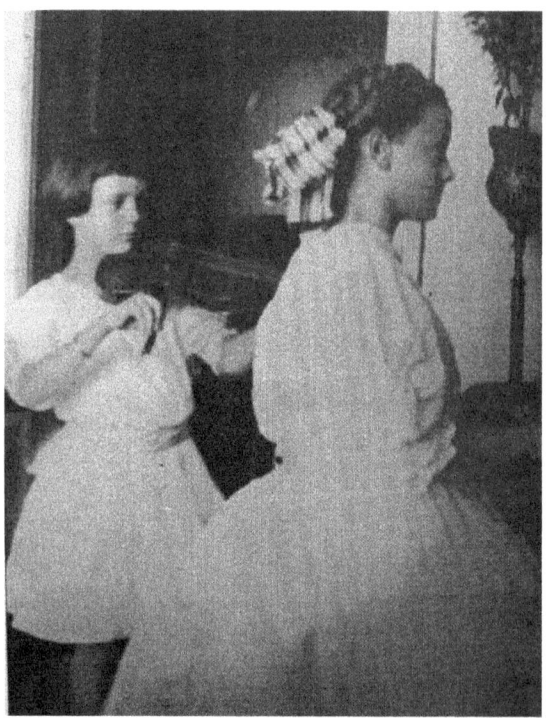

*Sister Noelie's music students, Ms. Partridge on violin and Ms. Mularkey on piano.*

During the early twentieth Century, Fernandina was known as the "Newport of the South," and many wealthy Americans from northern states vacationed here. There are reports that both the wives of Presidents US Grant (1869-1877) and Grover Cleveland (1883-89; 1893-97) as well as Consuela Vanderbilt traveled to Fernandina to purchase the Sisters' world-renowned, French lace.

*Altar Boy T. Howard Kelly with French Lace Surplice.*

On April 28, 1908, the Right Reverend William J. Kenny, third Bishop of the Diocese of St. Augustine, visiting St. Michael's confirmed a class of forty-five youngsters, and gave First Holy Communion to a dozen boys and girls that morning followed by a gala attended by the community in Villalonga Park. St. Michaels Church and St. Michael's Academy are still considered, as they were then, highly respected and enduring historical centerpieces of the area's history.

The first Principal of St. Joseph's Academy, Sister Agnes, had a graduating class in 1907 of 62 students, including those who earned the title "Sister Agnes' Stars." They served to form a solid foundation for parish growth for generations.

*Sister Agnes' Stars*

The Star students in the picture and the names of many of those in the graduating class represented well-established families in our parish and community. Sister Agnes's Stars, (First Row Left to Right: Harry Johnson, Bertram Murphy, Gus McNeil; Second Row: Helen Morse O'Hagan, Theo McNeil, Marion Manucy; Top Row: Lottie O'Hagan, Alma Morse Partridge, Irene O'Hagan, Anita Horsey, Kitty Lassere, Jennie O'Hagan) Three O'Hagan girls in Top Row #1, #3, #6. Other familiar names in that graduating class: Waas, Kelly, Whitney, Suhrer, Klotz, Hernandez, Davis, Mularkey, Roux.

*Bishop Curley*

Michael J. Curley is named Bishop of the Diocese of St. Augustine at the beginning of WWI the "War to end all Wars" in 1914, overseeing 35,000 Catholics and a post-war period of anti-Catholicism and the first "red scare" with the Bolshevik revolution in Russia in 1917. At the time Curley was the youngest Bishop in the United States.

When Father O'Brian departed in the fall of 1911, St. Michael's found itself without a Pastor for a few months until the Very Reverend James Nunnan became Pastor of St. Michael's acting in that capacity until March 1922. Father Nunnan was born in 1872 the year St. Michael's Cornerstone was laid, in Ardfelt, County Kerry, Ireland. He was adopted by Bishop Moore, was sent to the American college at Rome to take his theological course and obtained his Doctor of Divinity from the College of the Propagation of the Faith. The college was established in 1627 to train missionaries to spread Catholicism around the world. He arrived for his first assignment in a foreign land—St. Augustine, Florida---in December 1898 to be assistant to Reverend Michael Maher, acting rector of the Cathedral Basilica of St. Augustine. Following Father James Nunnan's pastorate at St. Michael's, which encompassed the years of World War I [July 28, 1914-Nov 11,1918], he went on to become rector of the Cathedral Basilica of St. Augustine, and Vicar General of the Diocese of St. Augustine.

The Reverend John Fowlkes, SJ conducted a week's mission at St. Michaels, Feb 3-10, 1924, with the largest attendance of parishioners to date. In speaking of the patriotism of the parishioners of St. Michael's and St. Peter Claver's churches during World War I, "it can be truthfully summed up in these words: in every respect, all of them cheerfully 'went over the top' [a reference to their bravery in climbing out of the trenches or putting their lives on the line and confronting the enemy]. Some served in the Army and Navy. Their names are Hamilton Hersey, Lt. Col John R. Ferreira, T. Howard Kelly, Maurice Kelly, Henry P. Livingston, P.J. McCleary, Bernard Cone, William Suhrer and Anthony R. Brady." Also listed in the "Brief History of the Churches of the Diocese of St. Augustine Florida" contributed by the former pastor J. J. Nevin are familiar pioneer family names of St. Michael's congregation: Nolan, Lassere, Waas, Leddy, Powers, Villalonga, Ferreira, the Kelley's and Mularkey's.

During the pastorate of Father John J. Nevin between 1922 and 1926, the Church and pastoral residence were remodeled and beautified, and a new bell tower costing about two thousand dollars was added to the northwest corner of the Church and a new bell installed and dedicated. The new bell was called the "Raymond Bell" in memory of Mr. H. H. Raymond who made the gift of the bell possible. The inscription on the bell reads: "Under the auspices of the Ladies Circle of the Church this bell was principally the gift of H.H. Raymond. May Its Sound be heard Far and Near for the Glory of God and Salvation of Souls." July 2.1924, McShane Bell Foundry Co. Baltimore, Md. 1924.

*The Raymond Bell on platform*

The new bell was blessed on August 15, 1924, the Feast of the Assumption of the Blessed Virgin Mary, by visiting priest, the Reverend Bernard Weigl, of St. Leo Abbey, St. Leo, Florida. It replaced one believed to be an engine bell bearing the date AD 1750. For many years from the tall steeple, the bell tolled for the Angelus prayer daily (1), and the people of Fernandina set their watches by it. Sister Anna Josephine rang the bell every day with some of the layman until she was eighty-three years. old. Sister Anna Josephine spent sixty-five years of her life in Fernandina and died at age ninety-four and was the last of the French Sisters from Le Puy to be buried in Bosque Bello Cemetery.

Local legend is that Sister Josephine was so endeared to

(1)     See footnotes page 129

Sister Noelie who she taught music with for so many years that she asked to be buried at Sister Noelie's feet. According to the Archivist of the Sisters of Saint Joseph Convent in St. Augustine, Sister Noelie may have been a Countess of a very wealthy aristocratic French family and Sister Anna Josephine her maid and they entered the Order of the Sisters of St. Joseph together.

According to Father J. Nevin's writings, "the Parish organizations at St. Michael's at that time included: The League of the Sacred Heart, Altar Society, Ladies' Sewing Circle, Catholic Men's Club, Knights of Columbus Council No. 720, and, at St. Peter Claver, the St. Peter Claver Society organized by Father O'Brien for adults and St. Cecelia's Sodality for children. In the winter months, the Sunday Masses in both Churches are High Masses, in the summer months Low Masses. Benediction of the Blessed Sacrament, of course, is imparted at St. Michael's on Sundays and Feast Days of obligation; Lenten devotions, in honor of the Sacred Heart of Jesus…with Sunday school, are scrupulously carried out. Then also on certain weekdays the pastor says Mass at the St. Joseph's convent."

Father Nevins writes, "there were no missions attached to St. Michael's church at this time, but it had Stations which were in all points of Nassau County. "

*St. Peter Claver Church*

A new St. Peter Claver Church was being erected on the corner of Calhoun and Third Streets for the African American Catholics in the parish, replacing the Church in Old Town built in 1895 during Father Kilcoyne's pastorate. A very successful St. Peter Claver school that the Sisters of St. Joseph built to educate African American children on Calhoun Street. had eighty pupils in 1924.

The school closed its doors in 1959 due to the lack of students. The brick structure still stands there and now houses the St. Michael Academy Kindergarten.

## St. Michael's Parish

*Children outside St. Peter Claver School with Sisters of St. Joseph*

Father Nevin was succeeded by Father Thomas Jones who served as Pastor from 1926 until 1934. While at St. Michael's, Father Jones is given some credit for completing the construction of the red brick St. Peter Claver's Catholic Church started by Father Nevin and still standing on the corner of Calhoun and Third Streets. It was also originally built for African American parishioners and is in the National Registry of Historic Places and is now a private residence. An article published in the News-Leader, Feb 25, 2020, contains a number of photographs which were taken of members of the congregation at St. Peter Claver Church. **Prior to publication, these photos sat for decades at Waas Drug Store when it was located on Centre Street.**

*African American parishioners in front of St. Peter Claver Church*

Father Thomas Jones was succeeded by Father P. J. Halligan, a priest who was by all accounts loved by both Catholics and non-Catholics, during his lengthy tenure as Pastor of St. Michaels from 1935 to 1952. During his pastorate the stained-glass memorial windows were installed enhancing the Church's beauty and giving it an even greater atmosphere of religious devotion. He also ministered to the spiritual needs of St. Michael's parishioners through the Great Depression, the horrors of World War II, the onset of the Cold War and nuclear age and the Korean conflict. Father Halligan was born April 10, 1899, in Athlone, Eirre (Ireland), died on June 20, 1963, and was buried in Bosque Bello Cemetery at his request.

*Father Halligan and his dog Satan on his right*

Father Halligan and his lengthy pastorate was followed by Father Michael Nixon who served only a brief time before his premature death in December 1952. Father Joseph Ketter was then appointed Administrator of St. Michael's in March 1953 until 1957. While ailing, he directed the construction of a mission Chapel Our Lady of Consolation in Callahan in 1953, which has since become a vibrant parish with a beautiful new Catholic Church.

**Before coming** to St. Michael's Father Ketter had served many years in New Jersey where he had directed the construction of a Church, a convent, and a school. Father Ketter died on August 16, 1957, after a lengthy illness.

*Our Lady of Consolation Church*

According to a brochure and school prospectus prepared by the Sisters of St. Joseph and Parent Teacher Association (PTA) in 1959, "Prior to the new school term in 1957, Sister Michael Joseph arrived from St. Petersburg, Florida to take over her duties as Superior of the house [convent]. At a pre-school meeting with the officers of the PTA, it was decided that the students would henceforth wear school uniforms which would consist of a navy-blue jumper with a Peter Pan blouse, black and white oxfords, and white socks for the girls. The boys would have navy-blue pants, white shirt and black oxfords."

According to the brochure, "The year progressed nicely and came to a charming climax when the students presented the life of Stephen Foster at their Closing Exercise."

"The following year the Academy added facilities for the seventh and eighth grades, thereby bringing the grades from Kindergarten through the eighth. The present curriculum includes the following: Religion, Phonics, Arithmetic, Spelling, Reading, English, History, Geography, Science, Writing, Physical Education, Music and Art."

"Thus, the present Sisters of St. Joseph strive to carry on the treasured ideals of the first Sisters of St. Joseph, namely: *'Love of God and Love of Neighbor.'*"

The Reverend Salvatore Profeta arrived as Father Ketter's successor in the fall of 1957. He accomplished much working diligently during his pastorate to get the African American children to attend St. Peter Claver School, often it is reported, by procuring a bus and driving it himself. Despite his efforts, unfortunately for the children and the parish St. Peter Claver School was closed in 1959. In addition to his priestly duties, Father Profeta remodeled part of the historical parochial rectory, and the sanctuary and sacristy in the Church. Closets and cabinets were installed in the sacristy for vestments and sacred vessels; drapes and a large wooden Crucifix under a canopy were added to the sanctuary and new heating units were acquired for the Church and rectory. The large wooden crucifix is now hanging in the chapel of the former St. Joseph's Convent now part of St. Michael's Academy.

St. Michael's Church decorated for a wedding
probably 1950's
Lewellen Collection

It was in 1961 that the Sisters of St. Joseph sold their property to St. Michael's parish and St. Joseph's Academy was renamed St. Michael's Academy. Some of the Sisters transferred to the convent in St. Augustine and those few remaining kept the school open with the help of lay teachers until 1971 when the school finally closed at the end of the 1971/72 term.

When Father Profeta departed in 1959, it seems that some sense of stability also departed with him. As described in Captain George Davis's presentation to the Amelia Island Museum of History, October 12, 1992, "We must remember that prosperity did not return to St. Michaels until after the recession of the early seventies...we were a poor parish...with very few exceptions, problem solving priests were assigned here on a temporary basis to try to keep St. Michaels alive."

This might account partially for the fact that following Father Profeta's departure, St. Michael's was graced with seven different pastors during the following decade or so. As documented in St. Michael's church Baptismal Register, the names of the pastors are in order of their pastorates, Father Peter Reynolds (1959-1961), Father Michael Gannon (Summer, 1961), whose books are referenced here, Father Thaddeus McHugh (1961-62), Father William Holmes (1962-64), Father T. Leonard Duncan (1964-1970), Father Edward Kirby (1970-1973) responsible for final preparations for St. Michael's Centennial Celebration in 1972, and Father Bernard McGuirk (1972-73). Father Brian Killoran's pastorate extended from (1973-1979) followed by Father Thomas Sullivan (1979-83). Further confirmation of these pastorates is provided in a pamphlet offering a brief historical sketch titled 'History of Amelia Island from 1597-1972, St. Michaels and St. Peter Claver Church" believed to be written by Father Ed Kirby: "Father Salvatore Profeta accepted the parish records on 1 October 1957 and Father Peter Reynolds followed in 1959 and served until 1961; Father Gannon served only as administrator pro tem in the summer of 1961; and Father McHugh administered the parish from August 1961-January 1962. Father Holmes succeeded Father McHugh in 1962; he was succeeded by Father Duncan in 1964-70, and the present Pastor is Father Edward A. Kirby." Father Kirby served from 1970-73.

Captain Davis also lamented in his recollections about how during "the 'Sixties & Seventies' the beautiful Villalonga Park with its Victorian fence—the arches and arbors—and the exotic plants and shrubs brought from around the world that were cultivated and cared for by Sister Antonio" were removed and hauled away. Sister Antonio had spent much of her time caring for beautiful plants and flowers that had adorned the altars in the Church and convent Chapel on special occasions for many years.

*Sister Antonio*

The third story of St. Joseph's Academy with its mansard roof, dormer windows and cupola were also removed. That third floor was once used as the Sisters' residence and as an infirmary by the Sisters during another epidemic in 1888. All that remained in Villalonga Park was the Fernandez family cemetery and lovely

*The Grotto in Villalonga Park*

Grotto built in honor of our Holy Mother the Blessed Virgin Mary that was built by local contractor and parishioner Frank Mayer in 1950. Mother Antonio would have loved the Grotto but may well have also lamented over the removal and leveling of her beautifully cultivated park where she spent many hours nurturing flowers and exotic plants brought to her by ship's captains from abroad.

She was so loved and admired by the entire community of Fernandina when she died in 1930 all businesses and government offices closed on the day of her funeral and both prominent Catholics and Protestants served as her pallbearers.

Notwithstanding Captain Davis's reflections and lamentations, the vitality and vibrance of St. Michaels for which it had become well-known for over a century began to return with the pastorate of Fathers Edward Kirby and Brian Killoran. With the Centennial approaching, St. Michael's began to undergo a major restoration in late 1969 before Father Leonard Duncan departed; pews were removed, old plaster peeled away so that interior walls and ceilings could be repaired and painted. As part of the

.

restoration, new carpeting, a new organ, new pews and new statues were purchased and installed. New Stations of the Cross were acquired by pastor Reverend Father Edward Kirby from world famous carvers in Oberammergau, Germany home of the Passion Play.

During this renovation, Masses were celebrated outside in Villalonga Park. On September 29, 1972, citizens of Fernandina Beach joined in a Mass concelebrated by Bishop Paul Tanner, seventh Bishop of the Diocese of St. Augustine (1968-1979) with Father Kirby preaching the Homily. A dinner and Art show were among the activities marking the one-hundredth Anniversary. In 1973, all of St. Michael's Square, from Broome to Calhoun, and

# St. Michael's Parish

**Nature's Cathedral.**

*Mass being celebrated outdoors*

Fourth to Fifth Streets, was placed on the National Register of Historic Places, a distinct National Honor.

An article in the local *News-Leader* dated July 1, 1976, said, 'Today, Catholic life on Amelia Island is alive and well. There are more than 240 active Catholic families, while summer visitors as well as weekend visitors have caused attendance at Saturday and Sunday Masses to soar. Father Brian Killoran, now St. Michael's Pastor said he is 'especially pleased about the bicentennial theme of America's Independence, 'Liberty and Justice for All.' It is not only an expression of an ideal, but a reality in the hearts and minds of all individuals." With the approach of America's Bicentennial, St. Michael's people and its Pastor joined with other Christians on

Amelia Island and beyond to announce with great joy, "Jesus is Lord—God Bless America."

There is no question that the decades of the 1960s and 1970s were a time of change, upheaval, racial tensions, the sexual revolution, women's liberation, the Vietnam War, the Cold War and Cuban Missile Crisis with threats of nuclear annihilation. A Supreme Court ruling in 1973 legalized abortion and the killing to date of over sixty million human beings. Each of these had implications which we are still living with today. All this was accompanied by the assassination of our Catholic President, John Fitzgerald Kennedy, civil rights leader Martin Luther King Jr., and Attorney General Robert Kennedy, the President's brother. The Universal church and Catholicism faced major challenges in its relations with the "modern" world, prompting the Second Vatican Council convened by the late Pope Saint John XXIII in October 1962 and closed by Pope Paul VI on the Solemnity of the Immaculate Conception of the Blessed Virgin Mary on 8 December 1965. America and American families everywhere and in local communities like Amelia Island and Fernandina Beach were all affected by these challenges, as well as some tough economic times.

Captain Davis's characterization and lamentations addressed earlier actually proved to be pretty accurate. A Fernandina Beach News-Leader article dated December 12, 1978, states that "modern times were hard on the Convent and the Sisters who were transferred elsewhere, the third story of the building with its magnificent cupola

*The Academy without the Third Floor*

and dormer windows, was removed and the remaining school manned by lay teachers finally closed its doors in 1972." The article also said that "The Church applied for a demolition permit to level the building because it was judged hazardous, and insurance was an unnecessary expense."

It turned out to be a blessing that the demolition application was denied by the Historic District Council (HDC) and a solution was sought to keep the buildings. This solution involved restoring the Convent and leasing it to the Nassau County Council on Alcoholism and Drug Abuse certainly major social issues of the day. Through the patience and cooperation of Bishop Paul Tanner, Father Brian Killoran and the Restoration Foundation and its many fundraising events, St. Michaels Academy is still with us today. Once again, providence and the intervention of the Holy Spirit allowed the beautiful chapel and St. Michael's Academy to be totally restored to serve the educational needs of the parish and the community.

According to his biography, Father Sullivan arrived in the Diocese of St. Augustine in the early 1970s after serving in Korea with the Columban Fathers for a dozen years and as a seminary instructor in the mid-West. While in the Diocese of St. Augustine, he had assignments as a teacher to middle and high school students in Jacksonville and put together religion courses and wrote dramas for students in Middle School. He also served as pastor at area parishes, including St. Michael's, from 1979-83. Father Sullivan was born in the late 1920s and retired in 2007.

Father Edward Booth came to St. Michael's to serve as Pastor From 1983-1994, succeeding Father Thomas Sullivan. During his pastorate, Father Booth established a Pastoral Council in 1986 and introduced the Rite of Christian Initiation for Adults (RCIA) program, designed for those who wish to become Catholic or desire to return to the Catholic faith. It has been a very successful program at St. Michael's with some 363 individuals becoming Catholic and joining St. Michaels since its inception in 1987. During Father Booth's tenure, there were several construction and renovation projects which included work to stabilize the foundation of the Parish Hall, restoration of the bell tower and stained-glass windows. Some changes were also made to use the school and convent Chapel for parish meetings and leasing of the old convent to house the Barnabas Center. Father Booth also served as the Diocesan Director of Respect Life. He is also credited with writing a fascinating historical sketch of the development of Catholicism in Fernandina on Amelia Isle from 1777-1959 in preparation for the 174th Anniversary of the reestablishment of the Catholic mission and Chapel on the St. Mary's River. Father Booth's thesis was those Catholics who left the Turnbull colony in New Smyrna in 1777 formed the nucleus to reestablish the Catholic community on Amelia Island. Many of these pioneers were of Greek, Italian, Portuguese, and Majorcan heritage who made their livelihoods in local fishing and shrimping industries.

## Chapter Seven
## A New Millennium

Father Mark Waters arrived in the summer of 1994 to replace Father Booth as Pastor and was later joined in the fall of 1998 by Father Bob Napier, who became the first Associate Pastor at St. Michael's with both serving until the summer of 2002. Working as a team, they undertook several major renovation projects, including the restoration and reopening of St. Michaels Academy in the late 1990s and building of the current rectory on Church property on North Fifteenth Street affectionately referred to by parishioners at the time as the "Taj Mahal." Father Mark also initiated planning for the expansion of St. Michael's church to accommodate growth during his pastorate from around 400 parish families in 1994 to around 800 families in 2000. While the school and rectory projects were successful, the initial plans developed and presented to the Fernandina Beach Historic District Council (HDC) in 1999 and again in 2000 for expanding the Church encountered resistance from local and state historic officials and became a matter of contention for more than a decade.

As the first associate pastor of St. Michael parish, Father Bob Napier proved to be a gracious and energetic partner assisting with both the building projects and spiritual needs of the parish during this stressful and challenging time. Father "Bob" was ordained in 1990 by Bishop John J Snyder, was a fourth degree Knight and served as a diocesan Spiritual Advisor for Cursillo. The Reverend Neil Cornelli, ordained in Rome in 1937, was a resident priest at St. Michael's during part of Father Mark Water's pastorate and into Father Brian Eburn's pastorate. Father Neil died at the age of 93 in 2008 at his home in Michigan. Father Mark Waters retired in 2019 but continues to celebrate Mass when called upon to do so at St. Michael's and elsewhere.

*Third floor being added to St. Michael's Academy*

While St. Michael's Academy closed its doors following the 1971-72 school year, it did not become just another cherished memory. Just as the Sisters of St. Joseph first built it with the enthusiastic support and generosity of the entire community, so would it be resurrected in 1999. Through the efforts of Father Mark, with the intervention of the Holy Spirit and a community, it was returned to its former historic character and stately charm.

*Bishop Snyder and Father Waters dedicating Academy reopening in 1999*

Father Mark Waters was responsible for initiating a one million-dollar-plus labor of love with State preservation funds of $370,000 and donations from parishioners, local businesses, and a very generous benefactor. It allowed the Academy to reopen its doors in 1999 with its dedication by Bishop Snyder.

According to the HDC and City Fathers, it proved to be one of the most impressive historical restoration projects in the city to date beginning in 1997 with the addition of the third floor and cupola all removed due to deterioration in the intervening years. It also involved major repairs to historic chimneys, and new windows amid significant work in the interior.

*Academy with third floor being replaced*

Its doors reopened in the fall of 1999 as St. Michael Academy for K-4 with the help once again of Sisters, this time of the Dominican Order by the Dominican Sisters of Sinsinawa also founded in France by a Spanish priest, St. Dominic. Sister Elizabeth Dunn, assisted by Sisters Martha Rhode and Barbara Becker, acted as the school's founding principal.

Sr. Martha Rhode, O.P.   Sr. Elizabeth Dunn, O.P.   Sr. Barbara Becker, O.P.

*Dominican Sisters of Sinsinawa*

With additional improvements during Father Brian Eburn's and Father Jose Kallukalam's pastorates, it has now finally been returned to its once magnificent state after twenty-five years of disuse. The former St. Peter Claver school building on Calhoun Street. between Fifth and Sixth Streets was renovated and used for the kindergarten.

The Right Reverend Victor B. Galeone is named bishop (August 21, 2001) less than a month before the horrific terrorist attacks on the US homeland in New York, Washington, DC, and Shanksville, PA. He led the diocese through the aftermath of 9/11 and the 2008 Economic crisis. The man chosen to be the diocese's first Bishop of the twenty-first Century had no desire to be a bishop but would have instead spent his time in the mission fields of Peru where he ministered for eleven years with the Society of St. James the Apostle during the 1970s and early 1980s. Bishop Galeone grew up in a tight-knit Italian family in the Archdiocese of Baltimore, where he served as a priest in several parishes. Bishop Galeone was in the midst of his first staff meeting on September 11, 2001, when he received word that the United States was under attack by terrorists.

Fathers Brian Eburn (2002-2010) and Father Jose Kallukalam (2011-Present) were both assigned to St. Michael's by Bishop Galeone. They and their Parish Pastoral Councils and parishioners continued the "good fight" to keep the dream and requirement for an expanded and renovated St. Michael's Church alive. The continuing growth of the parish necessitated the pursuit of this dream, with the number of parish families surging in this Millennium from around 800 to 1,667 as of August 2021. Multiple parish surveys to determine the desires of parishioners, old and new, were conducted. To no one's surprise, there are always those who will insist that such historic renovations cannot be accomplished without "destroying the old." As a result, multiple plans were developed, shared with parishioners, and presented to the HDC, denied, and appealed and hearings held with the Fernandina Beach City Council (FBCC).

Parish Business Manager Tom Hable led the charge through it all with proposals and appeals and back to the HDC and on it went---too many to elaborate on with much more to discuss regarding so many other accomplishments of both Father Brian and Father Jose and their faithful supporters which must be shared. In conclusion, this experience underscores that nothing happens by chance, the final solution is seldom what "we" think it should be, but providence and pursuing what is best for all concerned and being faithful to doing what is right for the common good, and God's will be done.

> *Jesus said to them, "Have you never read in the Scriptures:*
> *'The stone that the builders rejected has become the cornerstone.*
> *This was the Lord's doing, and it is marvelous in our eyes"* --
> **Mathew 21:42**

*Father Brian Eburn*

Father Brian Eburn wasted little time upon arriving at St. Michael's, continuing improvements to St Michael's Church and Academy. He continued the planning and initiatives begun by Father Mark Waters to address the need for a larger church to accommodate the growing number of St Michael's parishioners. Born in Nairobi, Kenya, educated by the Holy Ghost Fathers, once ordained he returned to Kenya for ten years before returning to the states in 1973. He served in parishes in New York, Jacksonville, and Crescent City Florida, before coming to St. Michael's in 2002.

An Article in the Nassau Neighbors, Saturday, February 22, 2003, reported that "The Sisters of Saint Joseph (SSJ) returned in 2003 to restore the stained-glass windows, the first step in the grand remodeling of the Church and school approved by the HDC. Longtime parishioner Kevin McCarthy presented the revised expansion plans, both of which were approved. Sisters Diane Couture and Sister Lyn Payette had been in the stained-glass window business for twenty-three years and spent six months restoring the sixteen, ten by three-foot windows handcrafted in Europe" ... and installed in the mid-1930s during Father Halligan's pastorate. McCarthy, was quoted stating that the Church was glad to bring the Sisters of St. Joseph back, "they were so much a part of this Church, part of the history of this island." He also explained that "the Church and school expansion will coincide with the overall restoration of the 130-year-old sanctuary, which needs substantial structural repairs."

In 2004/2005 the addition to the middle school of St. Michaels Academy was completed. Architect Jose Miranda headed the school project which added a two-story classroom structure to the southeast corner of the existing school to house sixth to eighth grade classes. The first renovation and upgrade of St. Michael's Church was completed with the sacristy enlarged and side entrance and additional restrooms added. More work on the school was needed with mansard roof shingles replaced and the entire deck areas of the Academy replaced except for that of the new Middle School addition. In 2008/09 deteriorating upper sections of the historic chimneys at the school had to be removed and all original brickwork resealed. In 2010, the first major repairs were also required to fix a leaking skylight and roof at the rectory on North Fifteenth Street. A little piece of history that not many could or would 'remember' is that the bricks used in the construction of St. Joseph's Academy and Convent were transported freight-free, via schooner, from Philadelphia, Pa. between 1880 and 1882.

Another one of the many parish surveys was conducted with a plan developed to build a new St. Michaels Church on the mainland on Church property off old Nassauville Road at a cost of over seven million dollars but the economy collapsed in 2007/08 and the plan had to be abandoned. The short-term alternative in 2007 was to rent space from the United Methodist Church in Yulee with a 4 p.m. Saturday Vigil Mass arranged for local Catholic residents.

With the support and approval of Bishop Galeone and following the advice of Father Mike Morgan, Diocesan Chancellor "to plant a flag anywhere in Yulee to build a Church," a 15-acre parcel was purchased in 2010 directly across A1A from the Methodist Church and a site plan was later submitted and approved to build a mission Church.

Father Brian was assisted during his entire pastorate by Reverend Father Gerald "Gerry" O'Shea a retired Lieutenant Commander, Navy Chaplains Corps from Jacksonville, assigned

*Father Gerald O'Shea*

by Msgr. Vincent Haut, Vicar General of the Diocese of St. Augustine to serve until Father Eburn arrived. However, Father

Gerry never left his service with St. Michael's until his death in October 2016. Thankfully, Father Gerry was able to participate in the dedication of the new St. Michael's church as a concelebrant along with Pastor Father Jose Kallukalam, and Former Pastor Father Mark Waters with Bishop Felipe Estevez on 1 August 2015. Father Gerry also got to celebrate his fifty-year Anniversary as an ordained priest in May 2016.

*Deacon Art, Father Jose, Bishop Estevez, and Father Gerry*

He will always be remembered for his humility, wit, and sense of humor with his Homilies incorporating characters from the Sunday comics---Hagar the Barbarian, Sgt. Snorkel, Little Abner, and Snoopy---he had a car full of them. Those who served with him and knew him as a shipmate will never forget his favorite tune, "Jesus in the morning, Jesus at the noontime, Jesus when the sun goes down."

Father George A. Burns was a resident priest with Father Brian arriving in 2006. Father Burns served as pastor in the Methodist and Episcopal churches for fifty-seven years and was an interim priest at St. Peters Episcopal Church in Fernandina. He was converted to Catholicism and was ordained a Catholic priest on May 6, 2006. He served the parishioners of St. Michael's until his death on November 16, 2008.

*Sister Bridie Ryan*

Sister Bridie Ryan served as Father Brian's Pastoral Associate and graced us at Mass singing with the choir in the "old balcony" accompanied by the old pipe organ playing in the background. She retired, and parishioners bid her farewell in July

2014. She went home to Tipperary, Ireland, where she began her many years of faithful service. At this time St. Michael's was in the early stages of renovation, with the pews, already removed and on their way to St. Catherine's in Spanish town, Jamaica, our sister parish.

*Chapter Eight*

## A Decade of Change, Challenges, and Opportunities

The Reverend Jose Kallukalam was assigned to St. Michael's parish by Bishop Galeone and began his pastorate on January 1, 2011.

*Father Jose* **Kallukalam**

The records and responsibilities of the rapidly growing and diverse parish could not have been turned over to a humbler and yet confident, energetic, and dedicated servant of Christ. The more you get to know Father Jose, the more you realize how patient and caring he is about all his parishioners, and like a good shepherd, he will go the extra mile to care for all his flock.

    The transition with his predecessor was seamless. Father Jose immediately set out to take the church and parish ministries from being "good" to being "great." He did this with the benefit of an experienced and supportive staff and Parish Council.

    Father Jose was born, educated, and ordained a diocesan priest in Kerala, India, on December 23, 1972. He served in several parishes in Kerala before being assigned to Chicago, Illinois by his Bishop, where he attended Loyola University and earned a master's degree in religious communication. Father Jose returned to his home diocese in India for several years, where he was responsible for the production of Catholic TV programming, stage shows, musicals, and diocesan publications. He returned to the states in the year 2000, serving as the Associate and Pastor in the Diocese of Corpus Christi, Texas, until 2005. When he came to the Diocese of St. Augustine, Father Jose served as Associate Pastor of Blessed Trinity in Jacksonville, Elizabeth Seton in Palm Coast, and St. Paul's in Jacksonville Beach before being appointed Pastor of St. Michael Catholic Church.

    Shortly after arriving, Father Jose Kallukalam with his Finance Council continued the good fight to keep the dream and requirement for an expanded and renovated St. Michaels Church alive along with other potential requirements. Between 2009 and his arrival, overcrowding continued to be a problem which he experienced first-hand. He immediately added a fourth Mass on Sunday morning, reviewed the results of parish surveys taken in the past, and conducted one of his own, confirming parishioners' desires and the need for a larger church. Father Jose then immediately established a "Strategy Team" to examine needed construction projects in the parish to include a new Parish Hall, an expanded St. Michael Church, and a Mission Church. All were recommended and approved.

Father Jose, after consulting with the Parish Pastoral and Parish Finance Councils, and the diocese, hired a local architectural firm to develop the plans for a new Parish Hall, and construction began November 11, 2012.

*New Parish Hall*

Engineers who inspected the building found brick column supports under the building crumbling and other signs of structural weakness, rendering any effort to repair the existing structure not cost-effective. The new Parish Hall was completed and dedicated by Bishop Felipe Estevez on October 16, 2013. While the Parish Hall was under construction, and with the persistence and tenacity of the Church's leadership—Pastor Father Jose, Business Manager, Tom Hable, Architect Jose Miranda, Finance Council Chair Jan Smith and Parish Pastoral Council Chair, Jake Gosa--the HDC approved plans for the Church expansion and several variances requested by Architect Miranda in March 2013.

According to a News-Leader article dated April 10, 2013 [quoting transcripts of the meeting in March], "the addition will expand the sanctuary [Church] over 4,000 sq. ft. and …double the current seating capacity of 289…for an additional 279 seats…for the 1700 families who are parishioners."

By fall of 2013, Parishioners began generously donating items and sending in contributions for the Church expansion. Many parishioners dedicated funds to pay for items such as the bell tower repair, restoration of the Rose window and statues of the saints. They also gave to purchase newly designed stained-glass windows, and pews.

Nearly 500 families contributed to the expansion fund. In December 2013, a member of the Parish Finance Council announced during all the Masses that the amount needed to get the construction loan from the Diocese was $300,000 and hoped to have it by March

2014. However, due to the generous stewardship of the parishioners, over $400,000 was donated in less than a week.

*Groundbreaking ceremony July 23, 2014*

Based on the pledged funds, the Parish Finance Council formulated plans with Miranda architects, and applied immediately to the Diocese for the expansion. A groundbreaking ceremony was held on July 23, 2014.

Thirteen months later, on the morning of August 1, 2015, Bishop Filipe Jesus Estevez celebrated a Mass of Dedication and Consecration in the newly expanded and renovated St. Michael's Church which was filled at its new capacity of over 500 parishioners. Along with Bishop Estevez celebrants included concelebrants Pastor Reverend Jose Kallukalam and Reverend Father Mark Waters, and Father Gerald O'Shea, assisted by Deacons Scott Conway and Art Treadwell. The Bishop also inaugurated a Year of Parish Renewal.

*Dedication Mass with Bishop Estevez elevating the Eucharist*

Mr. Thomas Hable, who played a vital role as business manager and dealt with the HDC in making the expansion a reality, had the honor of presenting the Key to the church to Bishop Estevez before his resignation.

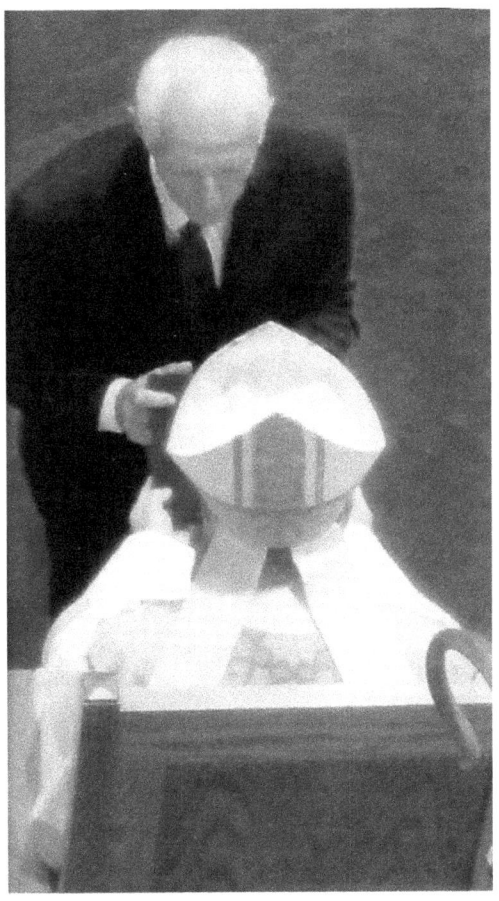

*Business Manager Tom Hable presenting Bishop Estevez the key to the church*

Bishop Estevez stated during his Homily, "...this is an important event in the life and history of your historic city. It stands as a permanent manifestation of the growth of the Catholic presence in Fernandina." This beautiful Church stands as testimony to the dedicated leadership of Father Jose, his competent staff, and generous benefactors, he wrote in the dedication program. "Now the entire community can rejoice over the magnificent offerings to the Lord."

*Stained-Glass window of the Resurrection*

Following the mass, grateful and joyful parishioners, attended a reception in the Parish Hall. Father Jose Kallukalam, St.

Michael's pastor, said, "the expanded Church exceeds everyone's dreams."

A description of some of the exceptional features of the newly renovated and expanded Church was offered in an article in the Fernandina Beach News-Leader on August 14, 2015, by Vice Chair of the Parish Pastoral Council, Catherine Turner, who had a major role in designing the eleven new stained-glass windows which were made in Lynchburg, Virginia.

The stained- glass windows represent the seven sacraments, and the Annunciation, the Incarnation, the Baptism of Jesus, Jesus with the Children and the Resurrection of Jesus. The Resurrection used the original rose window. This window is the main window over the altar on the east end of the Church.

Turner was also responsible for designing the panel in front of the sacrificial altar, which features a carving of The Lamb, sitting on the Seven Seals. The design on the altar's front was carved in New Holland, PA. out of one piece of quarter-sawn white oak and is mounted on an oval of Carrara marble, the same stone used for the renovation, and that of the original main altar built in 1884.

Many parishioners participated in the renovation through their ministries and, where possible, volunteered in various aspects such as moving the sacrificial altar weighing several tons back into place an inch at a time. And some helped transport chairs from the Parish Hall to make room for the reception following the dedication mass.

*Altar of Celebration with Lamb and seven seals*

As some remarked, it was truly amazing to see so many parts of this enormous puzzle carefully, effectively, and expeditiously accomplished. There's much more to add to this historical record.

In 2014, while so many focused on the Church expansion and celebrating Mass in the fabulous new Parish Hall, Father Jose and his leadership team restored the historic chimneys adorning the mansard roofline of the historic St. Michael's Academy. In addition, they restored and replaced all the wood and windows on the third floor which had been removed entirely, and more than a dozen custom windows on the first and second floor.

*Fully Restored Academy from Calhoun Street*

Also, in 2014, the "yellow house" on the corner of Fifth and Calhoun was purchased by the parish with a private donation to the

*Yellow House*

school and has been converted for use by the "little angels" in Voluntary Pre-Kindergarten (VPK).

      Father Jose Kallukalam was also responsible for the creation of our new Mission Church in Yulee. Father Daniel Guindon, who arrived at St. Michaels in July 2014, served briefly as associate pastor but was moved to oversee construction of the mission Church in Yulee and was assigned by Bishop Estevez as Administrator on 1 March 2015. He also celebrated many of the Masses at the Yulee United Methodist church until construction on the mission Church was complete. In the Fall of 2014, a two-million-dollar fundraising campaign kicked off with hopes of breaking ground for the mission church in late Spring, early Summer of the following year. The campaign proved to be very successful due to the generosity of offertory collections by parishioners at St. Michaels, the sale of 2.5 acres of land to the county, and donations by parishioners on and off the island to purchase significant items for the Church like the altar, ambo, stained-glass windows, stations of the Cross, sacred vessels, priests' vestments, and the like. In an article from the Times-Union, December 30, 2014, "30 percent of our parish families, many who live off Amelia Island in the growing Yulee community, want to go here [to St. Francis] and they see it and are very happy," Father Jose Kallukalam said. "There will be a good future because we will see more people coming. It may not be immediate, but it is going to happen."

The groundbreaking ceremony was held at St. Francis of Assisi Mission Church on May 16, 2015, and the Church was dedicated on March 17, 2016. The Mass of Solemn Dedication was celebrated by Bishop Felipe Estevez with Father Jose Kallukalam and Father Dan Guindon, concelebrants, with several other local priests assisting including Father Richard Perko, and Father Christopher Liguori, Deacons Art Treadwell and Vincent Abrahams and others from the diocese. Also, adult altar servers John Pulsinelli and Paul Donovan and three youth altar servers participated.

*Interior of St. Francis of Assisi Mission Church*

According to data obtained from Church officials, the number of families attending the St. Francis of Assisi mission

*St. Francis of Assisi Mission Church*

Church grew from two hundred parishioners when it was dedicated to more than one thousand parishioners today. The one-story 7,700 square-foot multipurpose facility is expandable to seat 400. It includes a Sacristy, the Sanctuary, several areas for meetings, a Cry Room, Kitchen, and Adoration chapel. Pastors at the mission Church have included: Father Rafal, who was assigned to St. Francis as Pastor in 2017 and remained for three years. He was blessed to have Deacon Vincent "Vinny" Abrahams to assist him early in his pastorate. Father Rafal departed June 30, 2020, for his new parish, St. Mary's, in Bunnell, Florida. The mission church's current Pastor, Reverend Father Slawek Bielasiewicz, arrived shortly after that from his previous pastorate at St. Mary's in Bunnell. He also had served previously at St. Mary's in MacClenny, Florida. While in the seminary in St. Augustine, he was one of several seminarians sponsored by the St. Michael's Knights of Columbus Council 14295. Deacon Brian Campbell and Deacon Tom Healy assist Father Slawek with his growing flock of parishioners.

Meanwhile, at St. Michael's, the parish ministries flourished and grew during Father Jose's pastorate. The Parish Renewal teams set up their goals and action steps to prepare a Parish Pastoral Plan for the future. In 2016, the church held a "Parent retreat" for the first time with the theme "Our Family, Our Future" and began our "Arise Together in Christ: Encountering Christ Today," a small group community studies program. This program is very much like the "Why Catholic" small study groups that hundreds of parishioners attended.

In 2017, the church held its first Ministry fair in the new Parish Hall. All Parish Ministries benefited and blossomed as a result of the addition of many new active parishioners and the support of Father Jose.

Current ministries at St. Michael's parish are open and welcome the participation of all parishioners. They include Lector, Extraordinary/Eucharistic Minister for Mass and the homebound, Adult and Youth Altar Server and Usher/Greeter. Lay ministries are Respect for Human Dignity/Respect Life Ministry, the Outreach/Health Ministry, and Food Ministry. The Community Outreach ministries are the Interfaith Dinner Network (IDN),

Coalition for the Homeless Day Drop-In Center, Visitation, and Bereavement-Living with Loss. Also, parishioners participate in the church's Lay organizations such as St. Michael's Women's Guild, the Knights of Columbus Council 14295, and the Men's Club.

Several ministries require training or completing an online course and evaluations, especially those involving visitation, ministering to the homebound, or working with children as a Catechist. Throughout his pastorate, Father Jose has always promoted an atmosphere of inclusion and diversity. As such, there are many ways and opportunities as a parishioner of St. Michael's to share as much of one's time and talents as one may be willing and able to offer.

With the Parish Hall's extensive modern kitchen facilities, the parish came together to celebrate with the first-ever Dinner Theater, Father Jose's seventieth birthday, and a series of appreciation dinners for our ministries. Father Jose announced a plan in January 2018 to strengthen our families and family relationships based on recommendations from the Pastoral Planning Team. In October, the entire parish and community came together for the annual Fall Festival with its "Trunk or Treat" event and live music in Villalonga Park. St. Michael's Academy children regaled parishioners with their Live Nativity scene and Christmas Angels program at Masses during the Advent and Christmas season. These holiday offerings are destined to become a living tradition.

In March 2018, Reverend Briggs Hurley, who had spent a summer at St. Michael's as a seminarian in 2012, returned following his theological studies at the Pontifical North American College, the Pontifical Patristic Institute, and the Pontifical Gregorian University in Rome, Italy. He was ordained in June 2017, at the Cathedral Basilica in St. Augustine. Father Briggs served at St. Michael's in his first parish assignment as Parochial Vicar supporting Father Jose through the early stages of the COVID-19 pandemic and was reassigned to St. Joseph's Parish in Mandarin in August 2020. He often referred to his time at St. Michael's as his "honeymoon" assignment. Deacon Art Treadwell who had retired on September 30, 2019, continued to return to assist Father Jose when he needed him most.

*Father Briggs celebrating Corpus Christi with Deacon Art*

Thanks to Father Jose, the church also welcomed their own "Angels of Labor" In February 2019. St. Michael's was once again blessed as a parish family when, like a couple of his predecessors, Father Jose called on two Sisters of the Adoration of the Blessed Sacrament to join our Parish family. Both Sisters had served previously in Father Jose's home State of Kerala, on the coast of India, and came to St. Michael's just in time to help get the parish through the COVID -19 pandemic. Upon their arrival at St. Michael's, Sister Rose Paul Madessery became the Office Manager and Sister Josephine Thekkumthala, the new Pastoral Associate.

*Sister Josephine (left) and Sister Rose Paul (right) together.*

After earning her bachelor's degree in Sociology and Master's in Social Work, Sister Rose Paul made her Final Religious Profession. She began her social worker ministry in Kerala and New Delhi, India. She came to the States in 2002 when she went to the Diocese of Corpus Christi, Texas, at the request of her Bishop to serve as the Operational Supervisor for the Mother Theresa Shelter for the Homeless with the Catholic Charities for sixteen years. In 2018, Catholic Charities honored her with their "Best Humanitarian Award" for her service to the homeless.

Sister Josephine made her Final Religious Profession in 2015, earned a bachelor's degree in Theology and her teaching certification while in New Delhi. Before coming to the United States, she worked as a warden of a hostel for young girls and did pastoral work in Kerala, India. St. Michael's had been without a Pastoral Associate since the departure of Sister Bridie Ryan in July 2014.

Father Brigg's departure in August 2020 with strict COVID-19 restrictions in place left Father Jose to celebrate all Masses and perform other pastoral duties on his own. Deacon Art returned to assist him as he had on many occasions for Christmas 2020 and the Easter Triduum in 2021. While many churches were closed, St. Michael Catholic Church continued to hold daily and weekend Masses under Father Jose's guidance with the assistance of the new Business Manager and self-made audio-visual technician Walt Edwards via video streaming following all the necessary Diocesan and Center for Disease Control (CDC) health guidelines. As an adult altar server who happened to be scheduled to serve daily Mass the week of March 11, 2020, John Pulsinelli, the author of this history felt blessed to stay on and serve, eventually with Sister Josephine and a few other adult altar servers joining them for the long haul. Throughout the entire year, the altar servers employed extra cautionary procedures to protect Father Jose, the pastor, from COVID- 19 exposure.

Along the journey over the past decade, St. Michael's had a wonderful group of visiting priests to assist Father Jose. Among them were Father Gerry O'Shea, Father Bob McDermott, Father Richard Perko, former Pastor of Our Lady of Consolation. Also helping often is the now retired, Father Mark Waters, the former pastor who was responsible for the renovation and reopening of St. Michael's Academy. Monsignor Vincent Haut, former Vicar General of the Diocese of St. Augustine, is a frequent visiting priest, along with Father Ernie Davis, who recently retired from his last pastorate in Kansas. He gives Father Jose an occasional break on Mondays.

Additional expansion and renovations of St. Michael Catholic Church property and grounds occurred in 2020/2021

*New Parish Office*

with the purchase and renovation of a new Parish Office and Administration building at the northwest corner of Fourth and Broome directly across from the Church. This House was the one Ms. Leonilla Villalonga initially built for her niece, Ms. Edith Gordon. This acquisition turned out to be a most cost-effective and timely purchase on the advice of the new Business Manager Walt Edwards and Financial Council Chair Mike Mayer. Demolition of the old office building at Fifth and Broome Streets occurred not without some trepidation but mostly "tears of joy." Restoring and relocating the historic Liberty Billings house ("Green House") to Fifth and Broome Streets allowed for much needed, expanded parking.

*Liberty Billings House*

All this occurred during the COVID-19 pandemic. Much like the expansion and renovation of the church years earlier, it also required much planning, debate, and compromise with the HDC, residents, and other local and state government entities.

*Chapter Nine*

## Celebrating a Proud and Blessed Heritage, and laying a Solid Foundation for the Future

A state of national emergency was declared on March 11, 2020, due to the onset of the COVID-19 pandemic which caused the cancellation of many parish events throughout the remainder of 2020 and well into 2021. When the new 2021-22 school year began, the virus lingered on, and all students in the Diocese of St. Augustine were still required to wear masks. By late November 2021, many of the mandatory CDC and Diocesan guidelines had been lifted and were made voluntary. All are hopeful and praying that the parish may soon return to a full state of normalcy. In Father Jose's own words, "It was amazing that parishioners faithfully attended Mass by live-streaming and when permitted, by direct participation generously offering their financial support to the parish. While many parishes struggled to make ends meet, St. Michael's met its financial obligations and goals and kept up its spiritual fervor."

*Father Jose and Bishop Estevez celebrating Mass*

Bishop Felipe Estevez celebrated the Mass of Inauguration of St. Michael's 150th Anniversary on 25 September 2021, with Pastor Father Jose Kallukalam as concelebrant with Father Ernie Davis and Deacon Art Treadwell assisting. A reception followed in the Parish Hall and the author presented a history of St. Michael's Church and Parish to the clergy and parishioners.

As it is, history repeats itself in many ways, and nothing occurs by chance. While we have been facing the deadly challenge of an epidemic, much like the parish and community faced in 1877, we need only turn to one source for comfort and consolation, our Lord Jesus Christ. The energetic and thoughtful guidance of Father Jose Kallukalam and Bishop Filipe Estevez guided the parish through the many challenges of the past decade. Parishioners openly express gratitude and pride in the foundation that the church has laid, the paths that have been cleared for the future of St. Michael's Catholic Church and parish, and future generations of children attending St. Michael's Academy.

*Children with Cardinal, Bishop Estevez, Father Jose and the Sisters in front of the Church altar Columbus Day*

St. Michael's was honored with a surprise visit by Cardinal Carlos Osoro Sierra, Archbishop of Madrid, Spain, and Bishop Estevez on October 11, 2021. Cardinal Osoro Sierra represented Pope Francis at the Canonical Coronation of Our Lady of La Leche and Child Jesus on October 10, 2021 at the Cathedral Basilica of St. Augustine. It was a generous and beautiful gesture to recognize St. Michael's Parish during its 150th Anniversary celebration and the children who are the future of our parish, community, and America.

## St. Michael's Catholic Church Recorded Data as of November 23, 2021

Numbers in early years include both St. Michaels and St. Peter Claver Catholic Churches

Parish Families: 1,700 +
Active Parishioners: 4,278

Marriages 1860 to Present: 1,650
Internments 1866 to Present: 1,750
Baptisms 1878 to Present 3,375
*First Communions 1922 to Present 2303
**Conversions (through RCIA) 1987-Present: 363

* Accurate numbers for First Communions prior to 1922 were not available
**Early data prior to RCIA regarding conversions are unavailable.

Captain John A. Pulsinelli, USN (ret)

## Acknowledgments

When our Pastor Reverend Father Jose Kallukalam asked me to write the history of St. Michael's Church and Parish to commemorate the sesquicentennial (150$^{th}$ Anniversary) of the "founding" of the church and parish, I was both surprised and honored. I was sure there were others more qualified and deserving to do so, and this history borrows heavily from what others have written on the subject in the past. I also owe a special thank you and want to express gratitude to parishioners Marie and Mark Fenn. Their professional publication and financial support made it possible to create this commemorative book honoring the 150$^{th}$ Anniversary of St. Michael's Roman Catholic Church and Parish.

I must acknowledge the tremendous assistance and support of Mrs. Ronda Outler, Archivist, and the entire Staff at Amelia Island Museum of History (AIMH), who provided me access to a veritable "goldmine" of historical documents, articles, and photographs, many of which I cite in this book and bibliography.

Other church and parish histories exist, and I consulted those as part of my extensive research. For those interested, they are *A brief history of St. Michael's Church* written by former parish priest Rev. John J. Nevin, published in 1933 by Abbey Press, St. Leo, Florida. *A Historical Sketch* by former pastor Rev. Ed Booth on the development of Catholicism in Fernandina and Amelia Isle 1777-1959. *A History of Amelia Island from 1597-1972, St Michael's and*

*St. Peter Claver Church* prepared by Reverend Edward A. Kirby and published in pamphlet form for St. Michael's Centennial celebration in 1972. Other materials and news articles include those of Willyne Blanchard for the Fernandina Beach News-Leader, and a presentation prepared by Captain George T. Davis, pilot, and Harbormaster, Port of Fernandina for the AIMH, all proved to be excellent sources of information.

Captain John A. Pulsinelli, USN (ret)

# Partial Bibliography of material reviewed to write

*St. Michael Parish,*

*Celebrating 150-years in Fernandina Beach,*

*Florida*

*American Indian Settlement to British Loyalist Haven, 1783-1785*, Popular Culture, online, no date. Describes how British Governor Tonyn used the port of Old Town Fernandina (called Hillsborough by the British) as an embarkation point for troops and Loyalists going back to Britain, 1783-1785.

Appendix A: Historical context and references, *The Historic Properties Survey, City of Fernandina Beach, Nassau County, Florida, Bland and Associates, Inc. 2007*

Blanchard, Willyne. *Centennial Marks Nearly 400 Years of History*, article in the Fernandina Beach *News-Leader*, September 21, 1972

Blanchard, Willyne, "St. Michael's Centennial: A Page in Its 400 year. History," October 8, 1972

Blanchard, Willyne, *St. Michael's Catholic Church*, article in the Fernandina Beach *News-Leader* July 1, 1976

Booth, Reverend Edward, *"Historical sketch of the development of Catholicism in Fernandina on Amelia Isle from 1777 to 1959."* Unpublished [prepared to celebrate the 174th anniversary of the reestablishment of the Catholic Mission and Chapel on the St. Mary's River].

*Catholic Directory Almanac and Ordo, The Year of Our Lord 1877*, D.&L Sadler and Company

City of Fernandina Beach, Florida. *"Stories from Bosque Bello-- The lives they led"...The Sisters of St. Joseph*, undated

*Convent Restoration Gets $1000 Donation*, News-Leader, 12-6-1978

Curley, Reverend Michael J., *Church and State in the Spanish Floridas, 1783-1822.*

Davis, Captain George T., *Presentation to the Amelia Island Museum of History,* Oct. 12, 1992.

Davis, George T. *St. Michael's Centennial Uncovers Spanish History, News-Leader*, 1972 (undated)

Davis, Suzanne Hardee, *Churches of the Golden Age of Amelia Island, St. Michael's Roman Catholic Church and the Sisters of St. Joseph*, pgs. 1-27

Reverend Father Jose Kallukalam, *Timeline of Activities,* January 2011-August 2019

Gannon, Michael V. *Rebel Bishop, The Life and Era of Augustin Verot,* the Bruce Publishing Company, Milwaukee.

Gannon, Michael V. *The Cross in the Sand, The Early Catholic Church in Florida, 1513-1870*, University Presses of Florida, Gainesville

"*History of Amelia Island from 1597-1972, St. Michael's and St. Peter Claver,*" Reverend Father Edward Kirby

*Historical District Council Call meeting, October 31, 1975*, to consider in New Business: "Application filed Dec. 26, 1974, by St. Michael's Catholic Church for a permit to demolish Rectory and Convent Buildings, block of Alachua block of Broome and Fourth Streets." ["Father Brian Killoran came before Council seeking approval of a permit to demolish the buildings." "Upon questioning from Council members, Father Killoran said 'the Chancellery felt restoration of the buildings was not economically feasible.'"]

*Historical District Council Regular Monthly Meeting, Nov. 5, 1975,* ... [a spokesman for the St. Michael's Church Council...said "that the church could not be expected to incur a debt to preserve the integrity of the two buildings along with its other financial responsibilities." "Council Chair [Andy Allen] reiterated...that as far as the Historic Council was concerned the permit for demolition was dead."]

Litrico, Helen Gordon, *"The Sisters of St. Joseph," Amelia Now,* Spring 1991

Roth, Father Benedict, OSB *Brief History of the Churches of the Diocese of St. Augustine, Florida,* Abbey Press, St. Leo, Florida, July 1933

*St. Michael's History and Father P.J. Halligan*, article in the *News-Leader*, Sept 21, 1972., authored by a church writer

*The Nun's Story*, text by Nola Perez in an article entitled *Why Amelia Island*, published in *New York Times*, Sept 15,1977,The Sisters of St. Joseph Archives, St. Augustine, Florida, author not cited

"St. Michael's Catholic Church--A Blended transformation," *Fernandina Observer News*, Aug. 31, 2015

*The Spanish Missions of La Florida*, edited by Bonnie G. McEwan, undated
Roman Catholic Diocese of St. Augustine,
Wikipedia: Official Site (http://www.dosafl.com/)

## Photo Credits

Photos listed below have been use with the consent of the owners / photographers

| Photo Credit | Page Numbers |
| --- | --- |
| Alan Young | ix |
| Mark Fenn | 27 (bottom), 105 |
| Deacon Art Treadwell | 86 |
| Tom Hable | 95 |
| St Michael's Church | 89, 94, 106 (top), 106 (bottom), 113, 114 |
| Author | 7, 19, 20, 25, 36, 39, 42, 58, 60, 64, 69, 91, 96, 98, 99 (top), 99 (bottom), 101, 102, 107, 110, 111 |
| Amelia Island Museum of History | 5, 6, 9, 11, 16, 27 (top), 28, 29, 30, 32, 33, 37, 40, 43, 44, 45, 46, 48, 49, 52, 53, 54, 55, 61, 62, 63, 66, 68, 71, 73, 77, 78, 79, 80, 82, 85, 87, 93 (top), 93 (bottom) |

## Foot Notes

(1) The Angelus Prayer

V. The Angel of the Lord declared unto Mary,

R. And she conceived of the Holy Spirit.

Hail Mary, ...

V. Behold the handmaid of the Lord.

R. Be it done unto me according to Your Word.

Hail Mary, ...

V. And the Word was made flesh,

R. And dwelt among us.

Hail Mary, ...

V. Pray for us, O holy Mother of God.

R. That we may be made worthy of the promises of Christ.

Let us pray:

Pour forth, we beseech You, O Lord,

Your Grace into our hearts;

that as we have known the incarnation of Christ,

your Son by the message of an angel,

so by His passion and cross

we may be brought to the glory of His Resurrection.

Through the same Christ, our Lord.

Amen.

**About the Author**

For fifteen years, Captain. John Pulsinelli, United States Navy, (retired), and his wife Sherry have been parishioners at St. Michael's Roman Catholic Church in Fernandina Beach, Florida. John is a career intelligence officer who authored his first book, The Politics of Deception: Target America, published in September 2020.

When John's Pastor, the Reverend Father Jose Kallukalam, asked him to research and author the history of St. Michael's in preparation for the 150th Anniversary, he was honored but not fully prepared for the task that lay ahead. Nevertheless, he accepted the assignment with the sincerity and commitment that he applies in all his church ministries as an Adult Altar Server, Lector, and Extraordinary Minister of the Eucharist.

Captain John A. Pulsinelli, USN (ret)

While not a local native, he approached his challenging research effort deliberately and systematically as he did during his many years of intelligence work. Through countless hours of detailed research in the archives of the Amelia Island Museum of History, he has crafted what he believes is the true legacy of St. Michael's Parish on Amelia Island. He has sought to bring that history to life. Though John initially described it as a tedious and laborious task, with the inspiration of the Holy Spirit, it quickly turned into a labor of love for his fellow parishioners, his pastor, and future generations.

Bishop Filipe Estevez, the tenth Bishop of the Diocese of St. Augustine, celebrated the Mass of Inauguration for the 150th Anniversary of St. Michael's Catholic Church and parish on September 25, 2021. The Reverend Jose Kallukalam was the concelebrant with Reverend Ernie Davis and Deacon Art Treadwell assisting.

The author presented the church and parish history highlights to the clergy and parishioners following the celebration mass.

It is the author's hope and desire that readers will find this book informative and inspirational.

www.ingramcontent.com/pod-product-compliance
Lightning Source LLC
Chambersburg PA
CBHW051827160426

43209CB00033B/1945/J